Endc

"*A wonderful exploration, but not only for readers to look inwardly, but to also look around at others, at where our lives are at, and mostly upward toward God's design and dreams for our lives. Love it!*"

– Cindy Coloma, best selling and award-winning author of over 15 books

"*You'll come away from this wise and insightful book with a clearer understanding of how you are uniquely gifted to contribute to the world, and why it's imperative that you honor your creative calling.*"

– Michelle DeRusha, author of *Katharina and Martin Luther: The Radical Marriage of a Runway*

"*TH Meyer looks at the glass ceiling the world has placed between 'creatives' and 'non-creatives' and shatters it. This those who have felt they are not creative, too timid, or simply too late to the life they were called to live, Meyer says, 'Pish-posh.' She delivers on her promise to help people embrace uniqueness, explore boldness, and encourage faith.*"

– Amy Young, author of *Looming Transitions: Starting & Finishing Well in Cross-Cultural Service*

"*In her book, A Life Of Creative Purpose, Tammy Hendricksmeyer [TH Meyer] is a trusted mentor, offer-*

ing us the tools we need to step completely into God's design for us as individuals, and as members of His body. Her relatable stories coupled with scripture inspire and ignite a renewed passion for pursuing not only our own creative callings, but even more, her words stoke the fire in our hearts for the Giver of these gifts."

– Kris Camealy, author of *Come, Lord Jesus: The Weight Of Waiting*

"A Life of Creative Purpose is a fantastic resource filled with thoughtful questions, stories, and Scripture each designed to awaken us to God's unique purposes for our lives. It is well-written, thoughtful, and engaging, an invitation to embrace our own eternally significant creative purpose."

– Cindee S. Re, author of *Discovering Hope: Beginning the Journey Toward Hope in Chronic Illness*

"In her book, A Life of Creative Purpose, TH Meyer masterfully blends personal stories with wisdom from Scripture to reveal the importance of creative purpose (even if you think you are not creative.) The thought-provoking questions at the end of each chapter will help you discover (or uncover) and embrace the unique way God has made you and inspire you to step into a life of purpose, meaning and fulfillment.

– JoDitt Williams, author/artist of *Delight in the Word of God: A Devotional Coloring Book/Journal for Adults*

A Life of

Creative

Purpose

Embrace Uniqueness. Explore Boldness.
Encourage Faith.

T.H. MEYER

Also get the FREE eBook:
Intentional Soul: 4 Ways to Purposefully Live and Love Your Life
Available at: www.tammy-h-meyer.com

Cover by Perry Elisabeth Design | perryelisabethdesign.com

A Life of Creative Purpose:
Embrace Uniqueness. Explore Boldness. Encourage Faith.

Heritage Meadows Publishing

Printed in the United States of America.
Copyright © 2016, Revised 2018
All rights reserved.

1-948797-01-1

ISBN 13: 978-1-948797-01-6

For every person who struggled or wrestled to embrace God's unique call in their life, from the stay at home Mom to the Missionary in a third world country.

To my best friend, my comrade in arms, my farmer-pilot-rancher of a hubby—thank you for supporting (and encouraging!) my own creative life.

Contents

When You Shred Your Life's Work

"The Spirit, not content to flit around on the surface,
dives into the depths of God,
and brings out what God planned all along."
-The Message, (taken from 1 Corinthians 2:10-13)

I HELD IN MY hand all my creative writing as I stood near a paper shredder in our apartment on the outskirts of a German village. I was determined to dispose of each lyrical line, every dotted "i", and anything I'd ever crafted from a young age.

Over my lifetime, only a handful of family or friends had read my work. I had cherry-picked them, both the words and the people. Few had seen the growing stack of closely guarded secrets I now dangled over the shredder.

When I was 18 years old, I'd toted many of these same writings to a window seat during my flight to Okinawa, Japan. I took the long trek to my new home, a speck of an island. As a teenage bride, I crossed large swaths of turquoise water with nothing but an endless horizon.

I carried my literary work with me, not risking them to suitcases. A lot could go wrong with airline luggage. So many unfortunate opportunities made it risky.

First, the precious cargo is loaded onto a conveyor belt, carried along the underbelly of an airport, led to an air handler who then (hopefully) loads it onto the correct airplane. After the flight lands at my first stop in Alaska, another different handler must transfer any bags to connecting flights for other passengers while I would've hoped my bag didn't get offloaded in the process. And then at my final destination, I would've anxiously waited at the baggage claim carousel.

Such procedures were not safe for an entire life's work—that much I'd decided. My pages could vanish into thin air, never to be recovered.

Instead of taking chances, I carried my little stack onboard and held it in my lap. My papers were safely inside the cabin and within sight. I guarded these lines of verse as if they contained national covert operations in need of security measures so as to not fall into enemy hands.

Now inside the cream-colored rental in the cobblestoned village of Bad Windsheim, I collected those same reams. The papers had aged and yellowed as I positioned them for obliteration.

I stood with the ebony-black, leather-bound folder where I'd kept them. I was ready to destroy what I had once so cautiously preserved.

I pulled a neatly pressed poem from an inside pocket. Pica font from an electronic typewriter dotted the weathered paper as I hovered the page near the shredder.

For the last time, I silently read one of my favorite poems filled with dark, Poe-like metaphors. It hid the truth of my life like a riddle. And soon, it would be gone forever.

I fed the first page between metal teeth as the motor vibrated to life. My hand had not shaken like I had imagined. A loud noise growled as the gears slowed halfway through the page like a monstrous Venus flytrap chewing a tasty morsel. Again and again, the 10-inch font descended closer to the mouth, each line of a poem or story ripped apart and consumed.

Also, in that pile of papers was the less-private work I'd done as a student publicly crafting pieces for classroom assignments. I had submitted one of the poems to a contest while I was in high school, and it had appeared in the local paper of the large city where I lived.

Another of those school pieces had been written during my punk rock angst. Hormones, Depeche Mode, and Billy Idol had filled my thoughts. My sentences and paragraphs read like a brooding teenage storm-cloud, mushrooming toward the stratosphere. But of course, I left out truths like sneaking into underground concerts by Black Flag and the French Ticklers, lest my own words betray me.

Long after I had grown weary and bored with that phase of life, my young words continued to veil what was really inside.

I even wrote a mythical short story for an English class submission where the teacher highly encouraged me to pursue writing. A fictional dream — that's all I thought of being an author or artist.

Writing was something other people did but not me. Fairy tales never came true.

And so I continued, shredder humming, as each piece vibrated past the narrow teeth. The last document entered the metal mouth, and I made a promise to myself. I promised to never write again unless I could do it with honesty and honor. I gave every line, every page, every poem, and every story I had compiled back to God in a pile of tattered strips.

At thirty, I destroyed my life's work of poetry and short stories.

I didn't know if I'd ever write again.

I didn't know if I ever should either. Up to that point, I had not been a good steward.

I had filled the pages with anger or sadness or darkness, not speaking to the actual goodness of life. I used writing as a way to hide my true self, like a mysterious passage no one was allowed to cross.

But as I stood there in Germany, one page after another tattered beyond repair, I gave each crooked word back. I let the jagged lines die. I came to the foot of the cross and forsook my earthly treasures.

And then I walked away.

In doing so, I left behind not only my words but also this life of creative purpose I'd always known. Not "creative" just in the artistic sense.

God places His good gifts in us and He gives them purpose. Even when we don't sense our gifts, talents, and strengths, or our purpose for having them.

Looking back, I see how my life cycled through changes by the decade. Every ten years or so, something in me shifted spiritually.

At thirty years old when I gave up writing, I started over with the birth of our two boys whom I later home-schooled. Through their infant and toddler years, I didn't have room in my life even to think about writing.

Around the thirty-five year mark, though, a small poem or two surfaced. I wrote some lines here or there, but unlike my former Poe-like slants, which evoked pain and deception, these poems cast out the darkness of my soul.

Yet there was no strong sense of a "yes" in them. Not until I was 40 years old, another decade after I had obliterated my writing in that overseas apartment, did the urge fully return.

Forty years old.

Forty.

Before Israel found their Promised Land, they wandered the same number of years in the desert. Before Jesus started His ministry, He was tested and tempted forty days. Before Noah rediscovered land, and ultimately, his saving grace, he floated on water in what seemed an endless number of days and nights.

Sometimes you have to let a thing die before it can be resurrected.

Sometimes you have to wait until God shows up and gives you that Pentecost moment before you have the power that you'll need to pick it up again.

Just when you thought your gift had received its final blow, God can revive it. He is a resurrector of dead things.

At forty, I knew myself better. I knew God better. In my 20's, I had given up my writing, given up its desires, and had given them to Him, only to discover that He would give them back.

I learned it's never too late to start again. In fact, it's never too late to go further than before. But once you do, fear will tower over you. Fear can stand like a mountain between you and that thing you've been called too.

Personal application & reflection:

1. Have you laid anything down, expecting to never ever pick it back up? What was it?

2. How long was that? Yesterday? Ten years ago? 40 years ago? What emotion did you experience when letting go?

3. Do you feel that God is resurrecting a gift, talent, or calling in your life? Or is there a new direction that He's calling you to imperfectly do? And what is it? Did you have any Pentecost moments of God breathing life into your calling?

Personal application & reflection:

4. What emotions do you feel in claiming where God is sending you?

5. What instructions do you feel God is giving you during this time?

If you're still unsure of what God may be speaking to you, sit down and write out 3 of the wildest, grandest, scariest things you'd do if you knew you'd never fail. Then ask God if there is any gift, talent, or calling His resurrecting or asking you to lay down.

*Then review your list from Chapter 1. Add the scary items and gift, talent or calling item to your list(s). Where do these things fit into those that you circled or * starred? Are their similarities or differences? Conflicts?*

One Thing That Strengthens You

"Let's leave the preschool fingerpainting exercises on Christ and get on with the grand work of art." The Message, (taken from Hebrews 6:1-3)

EVERY SHOP AND store closed at noon on Saturdays in the German village. Doors did not reopen until early Monday morning.

It is alarming how much you suddenly need to buy a gallon of milk or a pair of socks on a Saturday afternoon but could not. All commercial business was shut down.

We lived off a private drive on Dan Zinger Ring in Bad Windsheim. Green pastures, just beyond our backyard gate on the edge of town, were tended by locals farmers. The small German hospital would also be the birthplace of our oldest son.

During our stay in Europe, I spent weekdays staring at our concrete walls. The clock clicked on each minute over the dining room's coiled radiator as if the quiet roared in my ears like an ocean's tide.

On rare weekend days when the clouds cleared and the sun appeared, villagers spilled into the streets by the droves. Heads bobbed along sidewalks or park paths as people lazily passed the day.

Being an American girl, I had to adjust to a slower weekend pace. Stores, gas stations, or diners did not stay open 'round the clock. In Europe, I learned to live differently after being raised in a culture that is always "on".

I realized that rest must be done with as much intention as closing the shop doors and locking up for a day.

Before living in Germany, I worked like a busy bee. It was as if I entered a collective hive as I tirelessly delivered my contribution.

As a young Christian, I thought the motto — What would Jesus do? — exemplified the utmost amount of doing. Finish one task only to make haste and buzz off to the next.

I attempted to measure up with my work but felt lacking. Did I evangelize the teenage cashier when I handed her $7 in the drive-thru at McDonald's? Did I stop anyone in Walmart and share the Gospel? Did I feed enough orphans, minister to enough widows, pay enough tabs, picket enough social causes, or volunteer enough hours?

I'm not suggesting this is what the motto really meant. But the word "do" packs a punch in the church of North America operating in a 24-hour society. After living in Europe, I discovered that I take "do" to a different level.

As much as I love our culture, warts and all, Europe reminded me what it's like to purposefully take time off.

In our creative purposes and desire to do God's work, rest also deserves an appointment. Rest may even require a bit of pursuit. But in it, we discover that Sabbath is a sanctuary, a time of Godly reflection, of being.

As the world hustles and bustles in its usual North American way, there is the opportunity for us to be intentional. There is value and importance of putting things on pause.

When it comes to God's gifts, we can "Americanize" our output. Work hard, produce more, give better, fill the hole, and keep doing.

But overseas, I had to stop. I learned a practice of being and resting. And in that, I connected with God's Presence in the quiet, not in His to-do list. I learned to root myself in fellowship, not in programs. I learned to pay attention to His gifts and calling, in silence and inactivity.

At some point, there is a need to step out of the boat and into the storm, yes. And yes, we'll be required to eventually "do" what is asked.

But I've been known to also be impatient. While God reclined at the table and perhaps was still speaking – I've started without Him.

Got it! No need to say another word!

But eventually, I'd exhaust myself. From start to finish, I'd force myself to do THE THING. I'd wear myself ragged, burned myself out, and drove my tired bones to the brink.

Of course, we can face challenges or struggles when being obedient. But there's a substantial difference between a peace of God in the struggle versus full-blown anxiety trudging through a spiritual quicksand that sucks us under its cumbersome burden.

You sense it in your spirit -- if you're listening.

From Scripture, I've studied the concept of rest. I paid close attention to what Jesus did in the four Gospels. Of course, the miracles first popped off the pages.

But I saw another side not always taught in Sunday school.

Jesus went off and spent time away.

His popularity forced him to carefully and intentionally choose when he made public appearances. He spent time alone.

Jesus "went out and began to talk freely, spreading the news. As a result, Jesus could no longer enter a town openly but stayed outside in lonely places" (Mark 1:45, NIV).

He went away, by Himself to spend time with God and listen. "I have made known to you everything I have heard from my Father", Jesus told his disciples in John 15:15, HCSB.

God spoke, yes. And Jesus performed miracles, yes. He taught and He did "do" stuff, yes.

But He also stopped. He rested. He spent time alone to pray. He listened. He set aside time to do those kinds of things as well.

And He also enjoyed the simple pleasures of fellowship with His disciples. He savored meals with them.

They even sang songs together (Matt. 26:30, HCSB).

Jesus becomes a living example of purposeful rest, from God's own Son. Jesus did not work Himself into a frenzy. He did not exhaust Himself into a manic daze.

He returned to commune with God, even as the needy and oppressed begged for His attention.

From Jesus' life, we see that listening to God and spending time with Abba yields better fruit. And after this time, we discover He prepared us for our part in doing.

Doing can also be risky business. Holy and inspired actions require an ever-dependence on God, the Holy Spirit, and Jesus Himself.

We are not just marking tasks off a list.

And in it, I recognize my utter lack. I'm no longer my own. I give Him full access. I cooperate with His purposes as He directs my path. I learn to also listen. I learn to live like Jesus.

As you fellowship with the Holy Spirit, you develop an intimate relationship which enables you to "do" things you had not been able to do. Things that are spiritually enduring.

Remarkably, the same Holy Spirit who descended on Jesus and empowered his ministry, later filled His believers. When Jesus roamed the earth, His gifts were apparent and obvious. And even today, that same Spirit lives in each redeemed life. The same power available to Christ, now dwells within you.

Jesus touched and healed, and the lame walked and the paralyzed jumped for joy.

He spoke, and demons fled.

He confounded the Pharisees and priests with wisdom and insight.

He turned water into wine.

He walked and carried the Hope of the world with Him.

He imparted words of knowledge to those who desperately needed to hear.

He suffered and laid down His life.

He did everything the Father directed Him to do.

Through the eyes of Christ, God's heart beats for each of us. God's fullness was displayed through Jesus' life and sacrifice.

We do not glorify the gifts, but rather, the gifts glorify Christ by applying the power of His work in a fallen world.

When you aspire to live your life the way He lived, a complete picture comes into view. A life like Jesus is first an inward work before it's an outward one.

When you set aside limitations and give the Holy Spirit freer access, He embodies you. He empowers you. He emboldens you. He enlarges your spiritual territory.

He does the work in and through you.

In other words, the Holy Spirit does the work inside before it ever turns into action and duties on the outside.

When you start from the right place, you're enabled to do when "doing" is called for. The inner preparation has happened. You begin from a foundation, a position, hinged from the cornerstone of Christ's work on the cross.

Eventually, you learn to alternate between being and doing. You find clarity and intimacy with God in order to fulfill your earthly purpose of "do"ing His will.

You learn to enjoy your forced stay at home when the shops close. You walk past the train station and join the bobbing faces headed to the village park. You learn to turn off the 24-7 culture you were raised and listen to the roaring silence. You allow Germany to teach you how to live a different way.

You go against the grind and rest.

When you practice the act of being with God, it is the one thing that strengthens you. You may even discover a new path for yourself.

Personal application & reflection:

1. Have you been a What Would Jesus Do do-er? Has your "do"ing become more of a burdensome yoke than a light one?

2. Do you find it easy or hard to just be with Jesus? And why?

3. What situations make it harder for you to fellowship with God? Do you feel pressured to perform or work, work, work?

Personal application & reflection:

4. Where do you think this pressure comes from?

5. Have you prayed for God to help you relax and enjoy Him?

If you're still subscribed to the work-a-holics for Jesus club, look through the Gospel books (Matthew, Mark, Luke, and John) and meditate on the times Jesus rested and fellowshipped. Take note of place, crowds, pressures to perform, and other indicators of outside influences that could have drawn Him away from resting. Highlight every rest stop, prayer "meeting," and fellowship dinner you can find. After doing this, you should be able to redeem What Would Jesus Do, and give allowance to rest and BE as part of that equation.

{3}

The Fight for Your Promised Land

"Make every effort to confirm your calling and election,
because if you do these things you will never stumble."
- 2 Peter 1:10, HCSB

NOTHING WAS AS I remembered. The sixty-plus head of cattle were all gone. The hundreds of thousands of broiler chicks—gone. The round hay rings with brown bovine heads poking inside and munching—gone. The red-graveled road, where I had once learned to drive a bright-orange pickup, had turned into an unruly grass trail—long forgotten.

My family relocated to the family ranch. With years of disrepair, the pier and beam floors weakened with holes in the floor, and closets stacked to the ceiling with stuff and mice droppings. The 1980's security bars that covered the windows were rusted shut.

At night, I prayed for safety. Any house fire would kill us from being trapped in the rooms, no window from which to escape. The pastures sat fallow and overgrown like a match waiting to be lit.

Metal had long ago blown off the rooftops of commercial poultry buildings. Among the scraggly bush, scattered tin was buried like a minefield of a tetanus-inducing junkyard.

At the time, I homeschooled. Our two young boys were young and ran circles around me with their abundance of boy energy. I discovered the experience of raising sons was much different than raising a daughter.

We lived far from town, surrounded by dairy farms. Any store convenience meant the mere distance deterred me from traveling. I couldn't easily escape the conditions we now found ourselves living.

However, we moved here in obedience. God had burdened our hearts. We felt compelled to take on the task (of sharing responsibility) as a caregiver for my Granny. She'd once been a vibrant rough-around-the-edges Grandmother.

She had grown up during the depression. She kept everything and lived much like a hoarder. With stuffed freezer's, she'd keep food that was sometimes decades old.

But the parts I had loved about her, had also become the most challenging struggles in taking care of her.

Demanding. Spunky. Fiercely independent. Authoritative. Scrappy.

And now, she fought to stay alive. It became an intense battle within herself.

Fear of death kept her awake a night, afraid to fall asleep. I'd sit up with her until she'd finally pass out. But by day, she clung to life as if she had bear claws that could leave wounding gashes on the surface of life.

As she faced eternity, fear created a collision course with her soul. I realized how insecurity (when we've not been spiritually secured) surfaces when facing the fate of our lives. When the hot breath of death breathes down our neck, we are either met with the peace of God or with a terror of lost-ness. A terror that squeezes 'round the neck and causes our soul to gasp for life's air.

Inside her hoarded house, I felt suffocated. I was overwhelmed. I struggled to sense God. My environment challenged me at every turn, both spiritually and emotionally.

In looking for pieces of hope, I took short drives on nearby roads of black asphalt. I forced myself out, to recognize God's presence under rows of shimmering Elm trees or Oak branches.

After leaving the mountaintop where God spoke, do not expect the promised land to come without a fight. Don't mistake obedience to be an easy transition.

Many times, you will battle. You will take back your ground. You will recover what seemed stolen.

You will conquer inch by spiritual inch. However, that conquering may end up being much slower than what you had imagined at the beginning.

During this transition, I removed myself, walked outside the doors that seemed to close in on me. I stepped outside my situation.

And in each gaze of a bursting sunset of Texas sky, in a horizon lit in violets and deep cyan, you see how Creation testifies.

Only ten months after we moved, Granny would die in a hospital several miles from our house on the old ranch. But by the end of her life, we had prayed.

We had asked her about the condition of her soul. We had sat by her hospital bed and read psalms. Unconscious on her last day, we had told her how we could meet in Heaven, trusting she could still hear us. And after all her kicking at the goads of death, she had left this world—peacefully.

So many times, we can be blinded by our fears. We can fight the wrong thing.

We can get distracted by the little foxes spoiling the vines of life. Or we might not see past the littering mess before us.

We may hope for a better path from behind the thorny thistles and prickly briars that we find ourselves beating back.

Right before Granny passed, we'd begun refurbishing another abandoned farmhouse on the property. We stripped the walls of dark paneling. Scrapped the popcorn ceiling off the low ceilings. Added drywall with fresh coats of bright paint. Each window, broken and cracked, we replaced.

It'd be another three and a half more years of gutting rooms to studs and dirt ground that I'd pick up the pen again. I'd laid it down so long ago.

But I returned to writing as much with desperation as with caution. In my plight, I needed to look for beauty on a ranch that was nothing as I remembered.

After shredding my work all those years ago, I'd write again. And I dedicated my words to God.

When you're passionate about something, you may view it only as a "hobby". But God also utilizes your passions for His purposes. In fact, He most likely put them there in the first place

From childhood on up, I also painted with oils and enjoyed art class – my favorite elective in high school. I adored Emily Dickinson's lyrical verse and was intrigued by Edgar Allan Poe's dark, mysterious lines.

But as I grew up, I left behind my artistic leanings. Instead, I pursued a practical means for living and didn't have room for much else.

Yet, a time may come where we return to our passion in order to process life. We return to our craft, be it writing, or woodworking, or painting, or drawing, or tinkering, or crafting, or decorating, or yard work, or some other thing. We return because it gives our soul a place to breathe.

The curvature of country lanes wooed me to write of God's goodness. Roads shrouded under familiar Oak tree-tunnels or the altering shades of emerald green reflecting off a Bermuda blade, beckoned me to speak.

I revisited my creative purpose in life at age 40 even though I would not have labeled myself as a "writer". "Doodling" is what I did. Serious writers wrote books or magazine articles or published poetry, right?

My first-ever blog, If Meadows Speak, tutored me like a therapist. Change within me happened like thick molasses, sticky and messy.

My "doodling" included horrible clichés, masked metaphors, and ambiguous preaching. And it still does most days.

But whenever I wrote, threads of redemption revealed itself through the process of reflection among the heaps of trash that polluted this place I now lived. I learned much about myself as I pulled thoughts stuffed inside, to the surface.

Creation announced God's beauty whenever I stopped to appreciate it. In a sense, our gifts and talents also reveal

His work and artistry. Our passions becoming one with Him as He is manifested through us and reveals the beauty only He can create.

As I sit in the bedroom, the sun hangs over the sentinels of Burr Oaks and Elms trees. From my window, I watch clouds brighten the sky in hot pink hues. Crape Myrtles with their naked and spindly limbs stand out against the brilliant sunset.

God does not simply hand over our "promised land" on a silver spoon. We have to fight for it.

In our case, that fight was against locust trees with thorns as big as a butcher knife. It was a fight against decay, age, and disrepair. It was a fight against leaning fence lines and rusted barbed-wire that hung between Bodark posts like a dangling thread. It was a race to apply nutrients to pastures after the dry, wheat-colored Bermuda grass which is normally a golden-green, was shredded.

It was a fight that stretched outside my self-willed safety. It was a fight within my soul that questioned: would I fight to claim God's promised land (to include His purposes and calling) or would I stay "comfortably" discontent behind my walls?

Personal application & reflection:

1. What might be your promised land?

2. Have you felt uncomfortable with something was asking you to do? What was it?

Personal application & reflection:

1. What are some ways you might self-sabotage? How did you move past it?

2. What are some possible benefits of being stretched outside your comfort zone? What kind of positive changes or impact might it have on you and those around you?

{4}

Giving Yourself Permission

"In a word, what I'm saying is, Grow up. You're kingdom subjects. Now live like it. Live out your God-created identity." The Message (Matthew 5:48)

WOUNDS NEED TIME to heal. Before I attended a writer's retreat in 2013 (my very first), I felt like I was living in a frozen tundra. I'd just experienced the heart-crushing fallout among people I loved in the body of Christ. It was one of my hardest spiritual seasons.

Even though it seemed I'd been dropped off on a spiritual path to nowhere, I was not completely hopeless.

Jesus never left me. I knew this.

But my emotional landscape challenged me. I lived indifferently. No happiness or sadness seemed to penetrate a dark cloak I seemed to be wearing. I sensed a void of noth-ingness. Some might have called it depression.

I had wondered about that, too--depression. Initially, I detected that I was dealing with a winter of the soul that had overstayed its season.

But a word of warning about such times: they can be awfully hard to discern. I should've reached out for help and been more transparent. I should've told someone. However, once I had plunged into this icy state of the soul, I lacked the wherewithal to remove myself.

Yet God knew. Not that I had talked a lot to Him about it. My silence spoke volumes. I trusted Him, even then, but I had no passion left in me to plead my case.

In hindsight, I imagine the Holy Spirit interceded for me.

In *Listening to Your Life: Daily Meditations,* Frederick Buechner encourages us to see nothing as commonplace with God. Even if the purpose of that commonplace is hid-den from us, he states that there is still room to recognize God in it.

Once we tune our ear to discern His gifts and direction, then we're able to better grasp our creative purpose. Some-times our passions have been buried because of fear or from an idea that seems too childish now that we're grown up now. So we don't make time for such dreams or purposes.

But then, I'd run slap weary into myself. The last thing I may have chosen in my exhausted, near collapsing, end-of-my-rope life is to pay attention to it. To tend to the life I've been given and to nurture it.

Since childhood, I've been a caregiver. And I love how God knitted that purpose in me. But I'm also a fixer. I solve problems. I would cross valleys and move mountains if that could make things right again.

But life does not always work that way. And I can attempt to repair things in my own strength and sometimes to my own peril.

Being aware and noticing what's around and in you is one of the ways you can discern your calling in life. Perhaps, a passion inside you can also work like a compass needle pointing the way.

To know where your calling might be taking you, you may need to hush the world. Frederick Buechner talks about this in his book.

On my way to that first retreat in 2013, I traveled on the tail of end of a desolate time in my soul. Before leaving, I had considered canceling.

Caregivers do that. They quit on themselves. However, my husband said, *"No, you should go. We'll be fine. You need to go."* He did not realize how true a state-ment that was.

I'd hidden the fact that inside of me I carried this empty space that blinded me, even if temporarily. I had carried on with my usual chores and routines, like a robot mechanically performing predetermined movements.

Once in a while, I forced my mouth to turn around, into a semblance of a smile. But during this hard season, I didn't sense the joy in it. My usual mirth felt absent and vacant.

I recognized how far this had gone when I took a selfie for an online project. Like photographs in years past, I smiled as usual, cheeks pressed upwards into mounds with my eyes crinkled from the pressure.

But when I opened the shot on my phone, I saw something entirely different.

My hair glowed against the setting sun, striking its lightrays around my head, but my eyes stared past the camera, without a hint of a smile. My face displayed a wooden look, devoid of expression, matching the barrenness of my soul.

You don't always feel God. Your spiritual life doesn't always overflow with what feels like glory to glory. Instead, you may be left wondering how you got dropped off on some (spiritual) mountaintop. You try to remember the good ol' days that seemed just a short while ago. But instead, you feel frozen on the snow-capped heights where you'd once experienced God's glorious, loving Presence.

Yet, extending hope in the darkness is your faith. In a turbulent or disorientating blizzard of the soul when you don't sense God's direction, your faith can deliver you to safety.

What I realized when looking at my I-coulda-swore-I-was-smiling blank face, was that I needed permission to not be okay.

I'd been struggling with a loss of church and friendships. I'd been devastated by the absence of those I'd invested so much of life. It traumatized my heart.

Once you recognize your true condition, a condition you tried to ignore, you find yourself giving allowance. You decide to acknowledge your loss and to feel it. You realize you need to mourn.

You become aware that you had not noticed your need to grieve.

So I gave myself permission. I lamented over my loss and did not self-talk myself to, *"just get over it."*

I mourned the death of a community I loved. I gave myself permission to explore sorrow and to release it. Understanding this was critical in helping me move forward.

Not only do you need to give yourself permission to lament your losses, you also need permission to go be with God and re-embrace His calling, too.

When my husband told me that I needed to this retreat, he helped give me permission back to myself, to go take care of my healing. He delivered what I would not – could not – have given myself. And at that moment, he reminded me of Jesus.

My husband's simple statement empowered me to fully commit to finding sanctuary with God. I had to trust my family to Him in one of my rare absences. Besides, who am I to save and fix anything anyway?

Truth is, all you have is right now—this moment. Our trying to keep everything in order, working with robotic routines without feeling life, does not help us. And any fears that may try to stop us, do not relate to God's calling. They only relate to ourselves and insecurities.

Risk is scary. Making new friends and re-building community means taking chances.

But if we listened to our life, what might God be saying? And if we sense nothing, how might God be speaking in the silence? And what if we gave ourselves permission to wait without trying to fix it or fill the "void" with other things?

When you give yourself permission, you find healing and a God waiting to share with you, His purposes. When you cooperate in being part of the Body of Christ despite abrasive human factors or past hurts, it benefits a greater good for us and for you.

We need each other.

I need you.

I picture the Army poster of Uncle Sam dressed in red, white, and blue, wearing a top hat and pointing a long, bony finger right at me. But this isn't just the motivational propaganda: "We need you!" It's true that we need each other, but you also need you, too.

You may need to show up for your own life and participate in God's creative purpose for you. You may need to give yourself permission to experience all that God has.

Like a mustard seed, permission started with one small decision.

Living a life of creative purpose requires moments of authenticity. You not only recognize God's prompting, you also recognize the obedience required.

Permission plays a part in allowing us to accept things for ourselves.

We also can practice accepting God's gifts in us, to discover His plan and discern His will in how we are to use His gifts.

We can claim the path before us.

We can quit handing our creative life to someone else. We can quit hiding and stuffing it deep inside, too scared to uncover it.

However, after seeking God's heart, you will perceive your creative purpose and be able to declare them as worthy and realistic. You can accept the passion inside you. Then, you will be ready to partner with God.

Permission starts with God and is manifested when you acknowledge it. By the Holy Spirit, you are emboldened to not only discover His gifts and talents inside you but also how to use them.

He invites you to join the creative purpose He has called you too. Permission may originate from God but cooperation comes from you. And when you combine the two, God only knows where it might take you.

Personal application & reflection:

1. What hard things have you experienced recently or that you remember? Have you given yourself time to mourn those losses? If so, what did the process look like for you?

2. What did you learn from it? How could you minister to others going through a similar experience?

Personal application & reflection:

3. List three permissions you've given yourself. Or three that you've had to fight yourself in acknowledging those permissions.

4. How can you help others to give themselves permission to experience whatever spiritual season they're living? How can you encourage them?

Why do you think it's hard to recognize grieve, especially when there hasn't been a physical death? How can you take care to acknowledge grieve in the future? What other permissions, besides grieve, may you need to give yourself in order to fully embrace God's call in your life?

{5}

Called Into Discomfort

*"Let me tell you why you are here. You're here to be
salt-seasoning that brings out the God-flavors of this
earth."* ~Jesus (The Message, Matthew 5:13)

THE WORLD NARROWED into a silent cocoon of canyon walls. No cell phone service, no calling family or texting friends, or casual scrolling through Facebook, for three whole days. I'd given myself permission and now I was here.

Secluded among Mesquite trees and spring-fed rivers where Internet connections barely reached, I traveled alone. I finally entered the hill country of Texas in November 2013 on that first writer's retreat.

After the stretching years on our ranch, I was sapped. I'd reached the end of patience and hope in regard to ever seeing the ranch turn around and be improved. In the middle of the slump, I decided to go to this retreat and meet the blogging community I'd come to know over the years.

On a remote two-lane road heading to the lodge, I cranked up praise music from my smartphone and worshipped because Lord knows, I needed it. I pulled past the boulder entrance onto a dusty road high above a craggy canyon. I hoped to hear God speak again, to say something.

Anything.

I parked and moved my suitcase into my room. Soon, rain followed as the attendees scrambled out of the weather as we huddled inside a communal lodge on the first day. No hiking. No leisure walks near the Frio River.

Instead, we gathered inside the cavernous lodge near a large fireplace that measured higher than me.

A wall of windows overlooked the jade-green water. Off the balcony, bald cypresses, in direct contrast to the Frio below its reddish-brown needles, flamed in burnt-orange like a landscape set afire. It was as if the rocks themselves could go up in a blaze too.

At dinner over a steaming bread basket, I heard the stories of those sitting near me. I listened to their own struggles and saw God working in their' lives.

As if the light of a moon reminded me that the darkness of night could not be consumed, I saw a glimmer. My mood improved in a short amount of time. By the end of the three days, I left refreshed.

I sensed a new excitement for the future. A new purpose arose inside me, even though I'd known it since I was a teenager.

Remember, God patiently waits. Regardless of how we feel that we've stalled or gotten off track. Our creative purpose remains true rather it feels dormant or not.

And yes, our Christian journey starts with Jesus. But the keyword is--"starts." After we've begun, a whole new life awaits to be lived.

There are seasons for everything. A time to rest and a time to work. A time to mourn and a time to play. A time for caregiving and a time to self-care. A time to release and a time to capture. A time for doing and a time for being.

But if not careful, in today's social media barrage, you can lose sight of God. You might even lose yourself along the way.

In the book *Pray, Write, Grow,* Ed Cyzewski addresses the adverse distractions of technology related to prayer. He encourages us to practice being present throughout the mo-ments of our daily lives. *"We have to be aware that God is present throughout our days and is reaching out to us,"* he writes.

You can be lured away from your center of peace. Once you become aware of it, you can intentionally return to it through prayer and meditation, much like the writer's retreat did for me.

In doing so, you may discover a direction. Perhaps it is one you never before imagined or believed possible. As you develop discernment, you're better able to discern and know His calling for you.

You can live fully into today.

The word calling is not a romantic, unattainable, or mystical path. Rather, it can be the simplicity of faithfulness even in the most mundane way. Each calling relies on Godly obedience and personal relationship--no calling loftier than another.

In loving God with all your heart, soul, and mind, your truest calling rises. Communion with Jesus becomes your fertile calling grounds. Through relationships, you're compelled to operate in gifts, talents, or calling. His love inspires you.

For everything, there is a season. And whatever season you find yourself, necessary work and preparation is happening.

You can also look at discomfort differently. Instead, you can view it as a sign.

The enemy hopes you're immobilized by such dread. But that sense of unease can also spotlight the path of your purpose. The fact you care so much, may indicate that God Himself put that dream, project, or idea, inside you.

When you notice your most uncomfortable places, where you're reminded of your inadequacy, where you're shamed from being vulnerable, where you fixate on failing in front of "everyone", such negative attacks can highlight your call-ing like a wind-vane. Such intrusions can reveal where the Holy Spirit is leading and the enemy is resisting.

We know our weaknesses. Our failures or self-awareness prostrate us at the feet of God's goodness. But it also raises us in His strength.

God's creative purposes can come to us as both terrifying and terrific. As both exhausting and exhilarating.

There are no big or small sizes to callings. Nothing is too little (or too big) when called.

As I drove home from the retreat, I sensed more. I sensed God calling me further out of my comfort zones. I sensed hope and a fire in my belly.

I changed my former label as a "doodler of words" and officially embraced, "writer." I continued to explore what that meant despite my discomfort.

I allowed myself to be a creative observer of God's gifts and talents. I affirmed His purposes in and for me.

I sensed Him speaking. I sensed His still, small voice in my heart, just when I needed Him most.

During my seven-hour drive home, under a constant sheet of rain and stormy clouds, a series of creative sparks ignited. Ideas exploded like the flaming silhouettes of those bald cypresses sparkling against the Frio.

I sensed Him calling me again to uncomfortable places, ones that would require dying to myself (again) and letting go my need to hide and be safe. It both thrilled and frightened me.

Personal application & reflection:

1. What areas may you be holding yourself back in your own life? What is something you find hard to claim as a gift, talent, ministry calling, or other?

2. Take a moment and ask God, what does He want you to do with this gift, talent, calling or etc? What did you sense in your Spirit that He is saying?

Personal application & reflection:

3. Where does your discomfort come from? What is it protecting and why?

4. What if you went ahead and stepped out, although uncomfortable, what is the worst that can happen? What is the best that can happen?

Some things to consider: What gifts and talents is He asking you to unearth? How can you be a good steward of what He's doing? How can you develop more trust to give Him more of your life in this area? What parts of yourself have you not allowed Him to access? Are you being called to something you feel ill equipped to begin?

{6}

When You Are The Barrier

"Faint-heart, what got into you?" ~ Jesus, The Message
(Matthew 14:31)

WHAT IF I can't do it? What if I fail?

From that burning bush when God called out to him, Moses questioned God's instructions because of how he viewed himself.

In February 2016, I attended another local writer's conference. It was close enough that I drove to and from home, each day.

During the hour drive, one way, the distance gave me time to quiet my soul and allowed Jesus to soak me in the Gospel. I took these moments to remember the great I AM.

As I traveled to the conference, God dealt with me regarding a lack of faith. In the past, I'd relied on my capabilities, tools, and control. Fear had stopped me.

But isn't that just normal? To prevent yourself from being out there for God knows what to happen?

I also listened to sermons on podcasts. One in particular, *Foundations of Freedom* by Bob Hamp, helped to further free myself from allowing new fears dictating what I would or "could" not do.

Even though Moses knew his calling from the time he was a young man, he didn't see it come to fruition until decades later. When God approached a more mature and seasoned man, Moses still struggled to accept the call *after all those years.*

As we grow older, we learn more about ourselves. And sometimes what we learn reveals our own frailties, our own human tendencies, our constant need for forgiveness and grace.

"Who am I that I should go?" Moses replied when God plainly told him that he was sending him to Pharaoh to lead His people out of Egypt (Ex. 3:11, HCSB).

Even after God reassured Moses – *"I will certainly be with you"* – Moses responded, *"What if they do not believe me or listen to me?"* (Ex. 4:1, NIV).

In other words, *"What if they do not like me?"*

What if they reject me?

After you've spent years in denial or fear, hiding in a desert as you raise your family, you begin to think your calling was a mistake. Until that is, you face it once again, much older and more mature.

Your calling, gifts, or talent, may surface and create a struggle within yourself and with God. But the struggle may be necessary before you can make peace with what He's asking of you.

When God calls, you may ask, *"Me, God? Little ol' me--Me?"*

We can be more like Moses than not.

If you uncover your gift, maybe the one you've known was there but was too afraid to believe, you may think like Moses: *Who am I? Or worse, who will they think I am?*

God, in His mercy and grace, gave Moses a sign and a wonder. God revealed His power and authority by miraculously turning Moses' rod into a snake then back to a rod. Yet Moses still struggled: *"I have never been eloquent—either in the past or recently or since You have been speaking to Your servant--because I am slow and hesitant in speech"* (Ex. 4:10, HCSB).

I've said something similar, *"Lord, you know I don't pronounce words properly. I don't remember people's names. I stray off topic and butcher words. Don't you have a better someone in mind?"*

In the past, I've said "no": when "yes" was the correct, faith-stretching answer.

One year, someone called and asked me to speak at a women's retreat. Even though I had a message churning inside, when approached *without warning*, my gut-kicking reaction was "*no*".

I was too shocked to say yes.

Other women spoke much better than me. I'm not skilled enough. I don't comfortably stand before a crowd like other people I know.

I trip over words, overuse "um," use my hands when speaking, and tend to talk entirely too fast when nervous.

Not me, God. Surely You meant to pick a better speaker to go in my place. I need practice. I need eloquence, confidence, ability, and expertise.

Send a more qualified person, God.

But God expected *me* to speak. I should have been convinced by the Providential way the invitation appeared from nowhere. Besides, I'd recently promised Him that I'd go wherever He sent me.

He may as well have given me a burning bush. But because of self-doubt, I turned it down.

I had looked for an "Aaron"ess. I practically begged for one, when clearly God was saying *He* would be with me. My trust in my own capabilities or in this case, *in*capabilities, blinded me.

Afterward, I realized my error. I repented. I went back to God. I re-promised if He dropped another similar opportunity, I'd be ready. I'd say yes even *if* I felt *incompetent* and *deficit.*

Shortly after that prayer, someone asked me to speak. On *two* different occasions in front of a church.

Ask (in God's will) and you shall receive, isn't that what scripture says?

I said *yes*--both times. I wish I could say it was easier, that I was braver knowing God had orchestrated it, but I can not.

What I know is that God invites you too. So long as you do not become your own barrier.

When God stretches you, fear can be a tool that keeps you fully relied upon on Him. Fear can be a tool that requires your trust in Him. And then you must soak in the goodness of God's perfect love, allowing Him to cast the paralyzing fear, out.

Even as the months passed after my re-promise, even when I thought I'd learned my lesson, I discovered there is more.

I've heard it said, *"Where He calls, He equips."*

I do not doubt that God equips us. But the part I've wondered about in myself is, "Did He call *me*?"

"Who gave human beings their mouths? Who makes them deaf or mute? Who gives them sight or makes them blind? Is it not I, the Lord? Now go; I will help you speak and will teach you what to say" (Ex. 4:11, NIV).

"Pardon your servant, Lord. Please send someone else," Moses begged (Ex. 4:13, NIV). In other words, send a person *better* than me.

In spite of Moses' reluctance in his ability, God did not revoke His calling. It continued despite Moses' doubts, insecurities, and self-erected barriers.

Thankfully, God doesn't reject us after our first shaky no. He doesn't give up on us when we feel incompetent. He is not deterred when we feel more like a fraud than a faith-filled Bible character.

In fact, He gently pursues beyond our knobby-kneed, human self.

Driving to the writer's conference for two hours, I listened to the Freedom series. And God began to heal my self-sabotaging soul.

While at the conference, I met experienced writers who had already gone before me. I gathered courage from the path they forged ahead of me.

I told God I'd do anything He called me too. *Anything.* Speaking invitations? Yes. I'd no longer slam doors. I'd no longer think someone made a mistake asking me. I'd no longer assume someone had misplaced their trust in little ol' me.

Yes, God. I'll go. I'll accept. I'll step out of my own way and stop being a barrier to Your will.

Personal application & reflection:

1. When have you been reluctant in accepting in what God was asking of you? What insecurities plagued you like Moses?

2. How has fear stopped you in the past? Do you regret it and why?

Personal application & reflection:

3. What do you need to believe God for, in order to help you take your next step?

4. How can you better focus on God's goodness and love than on your fear or insecurities?

{7}

How God Reminds Us

"He has saved us and called us with a holy calling."
-2 Timothy 1:9, HCSB

OPERATING WITHIN YOUR giftedness means you point others to God. You can point with such intensity at times that your passion for Christ consumes everything within you.

"Oh, that my head were a spring of water and my eyes a fountain of tears! I would weep day and night for the slain of my people. Oh, that I had in the desert a lodging place for travelers, so that I might leave my people and go away from them; for they are all adulterers, a crowd of unfaithful people." (Jer. 9:1-2, NIV).

Jeremiah burned with zeal. He also wrestled with his prophetic gift but for different reasons than Moses. He saw Israel's waywardness and it broke his heart.

You want God's best for others. You want it for you self. You want it for your nation. You want to have all of Him, a personal, intimate knowledge of Christ. And you want everyone else to have it, too.

But when they don't – if they fall short or turn away all together – anguish fills the soul. You can become jaded. You can feel like giving up.

Your passion for others to "get it" can cause its own wrestle.

Exhaustion or weariness or even a sense of loneliness can creep into our souls. *"What does it matter anyway,"* we ask. *"I'm the only one. I alone am facing the opposition."*

Elijah felt the same way.

After God miraculously set fire to water to give Elijah victory over the false Baal prophets, Elijah ran. He *"ran for his life"* until he reached a cave and then lay down to die. When God spoke to him and sent angels to feed him, Elijah explained, *"I am the only one left, and now they are trying to kill me too."* (1 Kings 19:10, NIV).

Elijah had fallen into despair.

God didn't tritely pat Elijah on the head. He didn't shake him like an unruly child or quake the mountains to prove how big He is or how foolish Elijah was.

Instead, God bypassed the grand displays and chose to speak gently to Elijah. With a soft whisper, He asked, *"What are you doing here, Elijah?"*

You can be hiding in a cave, waiting to die, waiting on God, waiting for the enemy to find you, like Elijah. You can feel dragged down, worn-out from standing on God's word. You can long to lie down and be done, to let God take you into a tornado.

Let's just get on with Heaven, shall we? What are you waiting for, God?

We can become tired of this decrepit, evil world.

But just like He did for Elijah, God quietly speaks and provides for our needs. He encourages us by *reminding us of our calling and purpose.* He rejuvenates and gives us new vigor in our step to do His bidding.

At times, you may realize you've not stood in one place long enough to know what God might've whispered inside the cavern of your soul. Instead, you left Him standing at the mouth of the cave and set off on a journey, forging your own path. By doing so, you became a prodigal through the great distance you created between you and God.

I've done this. I've spent time away from God.

In heap of brokenness, I would also re-dedicate myself to Him. But I returned with a load of self-condemnation so heavy I was unable to look up. My burdens forced me to look only downward. I considered myself little more than a stray dog at the Master's table, begging for scraps.

For years, a negative mental tape played in the recess of my conscience, and if I had been more aware of it, I would've heard, *"Any good thing you see right in front of you? Yeah, you're not good enough for it. You're less than and damaged."*

It's ugly in there, in our heads. We can imagine we don't measure up to the next person as if we alone wear the brightest scarlet letter for whatever lie we've bitten off.

And when we do get the urge to return to God, those same feelings follow us and we feel disqualified, like we've been pulled from the race of being part of Kingdom work.

Let the better, shinier people do the God stuff, we say.

Peter knows.

Peter denied Christ three times during Jesus' night of great sorrow and abuse. The same man who, earlier, had vehemently rejected the idea that he'd ever betray Christ, denied Him three times. Peter understood the power of regret and condemnation.

What a horrible shadow to befall Peter after the rooster crowed that evening? What darkness of soul did he experience in the aftermath?

I've been Peter, too. I've abandoned God and lived blinded by my own strength, which really isn't strength at all.

I've also quit and returned to what is familiar, lulled into thinking safer is better. I've shrunk back, minimizing the risk of failure.

Mostly, I've failed to understand how God can raise anything from the shadows of who I thought myself to be.

Peter knew this too.

In the days following Jesus' crucifixion, Peter didn't bounce right back and start evangelizing. He didn't immediately become a firebrand for Christ. Instead, the weight of Peter's past hung like a heavy cloak shrouding his calling and purpose. **He needed a revelation of who Jesus was before he could firmly grasp *who he was.***

Just days after the crucifixion, with the night of denial still stinging his heart, Peter, along with a few of the other disciples, went back to doing what they had always done before Jesus came: they went fishing.

I imagine a sullen group of disciples ascending on the beach that morning ready to start their day. No slaps on the back. No jolly exchanges. Jesus' crucifixion still burned a hole in their hope.

As they went about their work casting nets into the sea, just like all the hundreds of times before, this time something was different. Despite their usual efforts, their nets stayed empty. They caught nothing. Not one morsel to fill their bellies. Not one payoff for their labor.

Suddenly, Jesus showed up. Is it any wonder He appeared on the shore in His newly resurrected body to speak to an *empty-handed* Peter? He not only appeared when they were hungry, He supplied them with food.

When we have nothing of our own to offer back, Jesus provides and offers to remind us of our purpose.

What did Jesus do for Peter during His first visit after the denial? Did he give Peter the side-eye? Did He confront Peter with, *"How could you? I loved you like a brother but you abandoned me!"* No. Instead, Jesus came to feed Peter, physically and spiritually, to not only heal him but to also equip and dispatch him.

But first, before they recognized Him, Jesus encouraged Peter and the other disciples to cast their nets again. So they went out fishing one last time. Why not? Up to this point, their hard day's work had not been rewarded.

As they returned the nets to the water, Jesus waited on the shore, not yet revealing who He was. As they hauled the nets back into the boat, the disciples discovered one hundred and fifty-three large fish clinging to the knotted ropes of their net. John, who'd been in the boat with Peter, suddenly realized it was Jesus on the beach.

Then Peter, who'd carried shame around his neck like a noose, jumped in the water and swam to Jesus. In the same spot where their sunken hearts began this journey – there on the coarse sand with the memory of Jesus' absence stinging in their hearts – Jesus returned and restored their hope. Then, in this very same place, Jesus gave Peter his calling.

My own struggles and internal skirmishes caused me to wrestle. A struggle that led me to remember my true nature in Christ. Only then did I discover my true identity and purpose.

It is a calling that never keeps you the same. A calling that continues to call you deeper into His plans and desires for you. A calling you find you no longer can lean into with your own understanding.

God encourages us by reminding us of our purpose, even one that leads us into the great unknown.

Personal application & reflection:

1. Which did you most relate to, Jeremiah, Elijah, or Peter and why?

2. When have you felt broken, tired, alone, or weary? What did God speak to you in such times?

3. How has God encouraged you lately? When has He reminded you of a calling, purpose, or gifting?

Personal application & reflection:

If you're still not sure what God is calling you too, get pen and paper, sit down, and purposefully ask Him. Write down even the smallest nibble that pops into your mind and make a list. Meditate on that list and allow Him to show you more about each item. Circle the ones you feel He's asking of you, right now. Put * stars next to ones you feel are for another season yet to come.

{8}

Knowing God And His Gifts

"Let's just go ahead and be what we were made to be,
without enviously or pridefully comparing ourselves
with each other, or trying to be something we aren't."
The Message, (taken from Romans 12:4-6)

I WAS RELIEVED. I had secured my place in Heaven and at nine years, loved what Jesus did for me. But I don't recall learning that God could speak directly to my heart.

I did not know that there was another way of knowing God, intimately and personally on a *daily* basis. I don't remember invitations to know the power of His Spirit--to experience the spiritual liberation of His *living* Word. A power that could enable me to overcome lifelong issues.

I'd only known denominations, primarily one.

To me, scripture was shrouded. It contained mysteries and parables. Verses were beyond my understanding. The formality of the King James' version confounded me as if it were written in riddles.

But as a young adult who'd rededicated my life, that began to change. Unlike my initial conversion experience at nine, this time I came with my whole *adult* heart-- mind, soul, and body.

Of course, at the time, I had no idea that a few years later I'd be standing in Germany shredding every page of my life's work.

In that initial phase of rededication, I only experienced God's amazing love poured out with extravagance.

And I wanted to know this loving God.

But how?

I decided to ask my Dad to find me a different Bible, a version I could understand. And that Christmas, he sent it to me.

As I read from my new Life Application Bible, I discovered nuggets of knowledge in Scripture, without a pew or pulpit.

I sat on my living room couch with no preacher or teacher explaining what any of it meant. It was just God and me reading together, empowered by His Holy Spirit.

The Bible opened up to me as if centuries-old mysteries were unlocked and deciphered. I understood not only the meaning on the page but also how it applied to me.

I came to realize there is more. There's always more of God when I don't suppress Him.

My spiritual life was reawakened. I feasted on His Word. It was no longer a legalistic requirement that I read. It was no longer a dry and dead manual.

Every word lived with promise. Every line — full of possibility.

Day and night, I absorbed the Word as if my very breath depended on it; each revealed truth was like air that breathed life into my soul.

I became unsettled, too. I saw God's goodness, yes. But I also discovered a God bigger than I ever imagined.

Growing up, I'd known the Gospel. I had felt Jesus' sacrificial pain and love for me so acutely within the walls of my childhood church. But something shifted after coming back to my faith as an adult. I wanted to better understand His grace, His mercy, His power to change my everyday life, and not *just* my eternal destination.

But just when you're being set free, the enemy comes against you. He draws the battle lines against you.

Old friends, who knew you beforehand, belittle you and can make fun of your "Jesus freak" transformation.

You witness a squashing of God's gifts. You may even see it happening to others around you, in your newly refounded family of faith.

There also are those concerns that gifts can be misused or those who believe a gift does not exist in today's world. Still, others refuse to accept a gift out of fear or distrust. I've been one of those in the past.

Yet, others may even accuse God's gifts as demonic. I tread carefully here because I do not want to mistakenly label the Holy Spirit's gifts as evil. That is a dangerous position.

I've also seen people discourage others from seeking any gift at all. Zip-o. Zilch. As if any kind of seeking derived from selfish gain and without pure motive.

Many years ago (before living in Texas), a group of us sat in our living room in a circle with other believers. A newlywed man sat next to his young wife. He was telling us about his passion to receive everything the Spirit had for him. As he talked, his voice rose in excitement while we too felt a stirring while he shared.

My heart was moved as I sensed the Spirit's presence. The hair on my arm tingled with an expectancy of what God would do and was doing. The man talked about wanting everything of God which in turn sparked my own desire for more.

Then an older gentleman, one who'd seen many ministries rise and fall behind dubious veils, spoke. "We must be very, *very* careful here. We should not seek the gifts," he said. He continued at length about the misuse of spiritual gifts and monopolized the rest of the conversation. He continued for so long the whole tone of the meeting shifted. The once fervent moving of our hearts became dampened.

As I listened, I understood his concern. I sympathized with him. Surely our sinful, human nature is susceptible to ego, pride, and self-adulation. We are all susceptible to such things.

But to suggest that we forsake *ever* seeking God's gifts?

I do not want to live with a quenched faith. I understand others have been jaded or spiritually abused. But I do not want to return to a powerless religion.

Besides, I believe God gives gifts in an orderly fashion, not to be applied any ol' way and cause unbelievers to think we are out of our minds (like Paul suggested in 1 Corinthians 14:23). I also believe the *fruit* of the Spirit – peace, love, joy, patience, kindness, goodness, faithfulness, gentleness, and self-control – is just as important as his gifts. Without these fruits, our gifts seem brash, harsh, and self-seeking.

But God empowered His people. He supernaturally enables us to display His glory. And God's gifts do just that. And as His children, we can open them with gladness.

I'm also reminded of, 1 Thessalonians 5:19, where we are warned to *"not quench the Spirit."*

Then there's Paul's actual guidance and encouragement to the church of Corinth to seek a particular gift and to beware of forbidding the gifts in others. Paul wrote, *"Therefore, my brothers, **be eager** to prophesy, and do not forbid speaking in other languages."* (1 Cor. 14:39, HCSB).

I've come to trust that God will not give me anything that is not of Him. I rest in that.

I no longer worry which gifts are His and which are not. Whatever is His, I'll receive. Whatever is not, I won't. The rest remains in His hands.

When you *pursue the Giver, the natural outflow from that relationship will be His gifts.*

I've witnessed the good side of this. I've known those of you in the Body of Christ who've sought God's gifts in order to love His body, better. I have seen your laser-sharp discernment and have benefited from your healing prayers. These people opened themselves up to receive *everything* God had for them—*as a way to serve.*

I've seen friends who loved Jesus. They didn't need platforms, stages, or up-front ministries. Instead, these seekers of God lived quietly and obediently in overlooked areas such as parenting, ministry confined to their own family and pouring into their small circle of friends.

They never once considered their calling or gift as minor or of little consequence. On the contrary, they poured their gifts and talents into their sphere of influence as if the whole world depended on their diligence in pursuing God.

And they sought His gifts. They expected to receive anything and everything because their hearts were set to serve Him. They didn't wait. They didn't feel guilty in their conscience for wanting more of God. They just got to work where they'd been planted.

God's gifts are not as much about *us* as we'd like to think they are. Oh sure, *we* may be blessed when we use them. Or perhaps our gifts force us to tackle our own willy-nilliness in a fight with the flesh 'til it yields. That *is* about us.

But it's also where we practice releasing ourselves into the hand of an almighty, good God. It's about letting go. It's about us cooperating and fellowshipping with the Holy Spirit. It's about separating the wheat from the chaff and allowing the Spirit to blow the dead pieces to the wind.

Your gift or calling may be hushed and hidden, quietly operating away from the public eye. Whatever that creative purpose is, God calls you to live it. Every part of the Body signifies an important role.

"Now there are many parts, yet one body. So the eye cannot say to the hand, 'I don't need you!' Or again, the head can't say to the feet, 'I don't need you.'" (1 Cor. 12:20-21, HCSB).

Your gift serves a purpose.

At times, operating in your Spirit-filled and creative-driven life frees up others to commit themselves to *their* callings.

For instance, in Act 6:2-6, the twelve Apostles summoned the ever-growing number of Christ-followers and told them to "seek out from among you" men to appoint over the business of caring for widows. This allowed the twelve to move forward into their calling and give themselves "continually to prayer and to the ministry of the Word."

Or look at Moses. He may have argued with God about his worthiness and ability to speak when asked to lead God's people, but we know how the story ends. Moses agreed. Moses acknowledged God's work and cooperated with Him to deliver His people.

Abraham packed up his family and moved to only-God-knew where, after He instructed him to leave. But Abraham's journey required cooperation with God's directive.

Like Moses, we can have an honest discussion with God about how we aren't the right person for the job. We can even list all the ways we're not good enough.

But Jesus said the Kingdom is at hand. Heaven is within us. His gifts benefit the Body of Christ.

When we encourage others, when we pray over one another, when we operate in our gifts, more of Heaven enters the world around us. We can hear from and *know* God. And as we are lead to serve in His calling and gifts, our impossibilities become possibilities.

Personal application & reflection:

1. Has there been a time in your life when you sensed God speaking to you? If so, what was that like?

2. Have you been discouraged from seeking any one of God's gifts for your life? If yes, what was it and why do you think that happened?

Personal application & reflection:

3. How might your gifts encourage someone?

4. What area do you feel God is asking you to trust Him more? Describe any time you have felt God spiritually sent you to an unknown destination like Abraham? Were you willing to pack up and go with Him?

If you're still unsure what you think about God's good gifts, you can take time to study two things: 1. Review Jesus' gifts in operation; 2. Start a study of 1 Corinthians Chapters 12, 13, & 14, Ephesians 4, Romans 12: 1-8, and allow God to define how that looks in your life. Add any scripture verses or key points here to catalogue for future reference.

{9}

Going Where You Never Thought Possible

"Make a careful exploration of who you are and the work you have been given, and then sink yourself into that." The Message, (taken from Galatians 6:4-5)

I WANTED TO BE a Spanish Flamenco dancer. As a child, I imagined holding cymbals between my fingers and making music. I imagined myself wearing a crimson-red dress covered in layers of lace with ankles showing in the front and a long flowing train in the back. Puffy sleeves would hang off my shoulders. Pressing against my ribs, a corset bodice would slim my waist as the bottom of the dress formed a bell shape, perfect for sashaying.

One Christmas, my mom bought me a doll that looked just like this secret dream.

In another phase of childhood, I pictured a life as a veterinarian. However, that quickly changed during my first visit to a vet clinic after experiencing the smells and gritty side of animal health care.

But one part of my childhood stuck with me. From very young, I wrote and enjoyed creating artwork. In high school, I sketched with charcoal and experimented with painting.

When one of my high school teachers offered me the opportunity for a small art scholarship at a junior college, I dared to dream. For a whole month, I fantasized about a career that I would actually love.

Before that offer, I had not considered college a possibility. I assumed I'd graduate high school, work full time, and struggle to pay my bills. End of story.

In the end, I declined the scholarship.

I don't remember exactly how the conversation went with my teacher. But essentially, I thought it too good to be true. I believed such lofty goals were beyond my reach.

When you've convinced yourself that your calling is less than possible, you do not challenge the *false* mindset. You do not pursue that calling within you. You do not know to push into what is uncomfortable.

Instead, you imagine this burning passion must be suppressed. Otherwise, it will torture and mock you as you work at a job you hate.

You do not think about being bold and trusting God with it. You do not realize that God puts such things within your heart and that means taking risks. You do not realize how you'll need to leave your old mindset to follow Jesus. That it will require you to forego your crutch, your perceived safety, and your best-laid (human) plans.

You deny yourself the dare to dream. Such a vulnerable vision frightens you. Instead, your buried purpose and treasures, sit like dormant seedlings waiting to poke its head above the hard clay of doubts and insecurity.

But in God's timing, you can live with both your passions and reality. You can cooperate with God to be all He has called you too.

I looked at my circumstances, my doubts, my fear of failure, my faulty view that it was too implausible and fantastic for me to accept such a good thing. To follow in such a trajectory, seemed out of touch. Daunting. Unrealistic. And too stupendous to be mine.

If someone had encouraged me to be ridiculously brave, things might have been different. But in time, the Holy Spirit taught me. The journey it took for me to get here today proved to be a valuable lesson.

And get this, you always arrive at your creative purpose *right on time.* Funny, how that works with God. His mysterious ways are not deterred with what looks like detours.

Had I started writing before God's timing, my fragile bravado would have held me back. My writing passion could've been altered or smothered by harsh college professors. In my early 20's, I don't believe I was prepared to face the risk of vulnerability. I might've molded myself into someone I was not, in order to please others.

However, after coming back to, and pursuing, writing I learned the necessity of self-examination and scrutiny. In time and missteps, I worked on the craft and practiced being true (and kinder) to myself.

Maybe you feel it is too late. You feel that you've run out of time. But with God, His ways and timelines are higher and different than yours. It is never too late with Him.

Time, distance, and personal growth allowed me space to have character built within me. Being older allowed areas to develop and mold me.

Establishing a firm foundation in my faith, I knew who I was and Whose I belonged. Time rooted my identity in Christ. And after I grew in that, when God called me into the "impossible", I went.

I stepped into what He asked of me. That doesn't mean fear was not part of the process, because it was. But fear was no longer a stop sign. Instead, fear humbled me and forced me to rely on the God of possibilities.

And what of those hours, months, *years* that I'd given up? I felt like Moses after he had spent forty years in the desert, living life as if the calling or purpose had been extinguished. When God shows up, you may see yourself as awkward as Moses. Yet when you're obedient, the journey refines you.

If I'd limited and restricted myself to a list of *comfortable* things, I would've missed the opportunity. And believe me, I'd grown to love my comfort, boring as it was.

Instead, I could've allowed naysayers to rule me. And if I had I would've never risked going where I never thought possible. I wouldn't have known the deep blessing of being stretched in my faith.

When you step into the unknown, you learn to trust God's judgment. Your faith grows in each step and struggle, in the attention and the intentional, in the uncomfortable places and refining of self-reliance.

How can we recognize the limitless possibilities of our life's creative purpose? Recognize God's presence in the awkward, hopeful, hidden passions and know when to step out?

You can open yourself to God and search. You seek His heart on the matter. You can keep asking. You can keep seeking from the same One who loves you and designed your life for His creative purposes.

You can remain on the lookout for where He's leading. You can be ready to leave behind ideas of how you imagined a "calling" should look.

You can go where you never thought possible when going with God. And along the way, you realize a deeper reliance. A reliance that asks, *"Will you go with God?"*

Personal application & reflection:

1. What is God calling you to do that takes you out of your comfort zone?

2. How might your discomfort benefit you?

3. Have you felt like God brought you an opportunity and because of fear, turned it down? If so, have you confessed it to God? Are you ready to take the next opportunity He brings?

Personal application & reflection:

4. List some uncomfortable things you feel God is asking you to say "yes" or "no" too.

5. What parts of being outside your comfort zone challenge you the most?

If you're in a comfortable place, it could be a season of rest and refreshing. While there, you can ask God to prepare you to go into the uncomfortable places with Him. Ask Him to give you a vision of where those places might be and how it looks in your life.

{10}

When You Face The Doubts & The Doubters

"Based on the gift each one has received, use it to serve others, as good managers of the varied grace of God."
-1 Peter 4:10, HCSB

I'VE STRUGGLED WITH shame and inadequacy. After living a prodigal life, I found it hard to forgive myself. I struggled to be set free from my former life. But then there were days I've felt brave, quieted by God's goodness.

Yet when I take my eyes off His redemptive work, when I fixate on my past, it is as if the Devil himself mocks and laughs. Condemnation pulls out every sin. It says, *"Look, at your guilt! It is humiliating. Disgusting. Disgraceful!"*

It pulls me down a rabbit hole, a skinny passage that narrows until it squeezes my rib cage and I can barely breathe. If I do not take my thoughts captive, I find myself stuck in a dark pit of condemnation. A shame that threatens to bury me alive.

But when I return to what God says about me, I'm encouraged to throw off the lies. By Christ's stripes, I've been healed. And as much as I've been forgiven, I also need to forgive myself.

When I realize I have the exact same Holy Spirit as the next person, the same Spirit of Jesus Christ, my perspective changes. I learn to embrace Him and all that He is calling me too. And when He gives me a revelation about who He is, I'm invited to be part of who He is.

One of my first encounters with a God-sized revelation happened during my reformed years as an adult. I was still a Christian babe who had newly returned to her faith.

I gathered with a small group of single ladies. At the time, I lived as a divorced, single parent as I gathered with our once-a-week fellowship study.

Usually, the group sat on couches. We would kick off our shoes and curl our feet under us.

On this day, I settled for one of the oversized chairs.

I don't recall the exact Bible lesson we were covering. But I'll never forget the spiritual gifts test we took at the end of that night.

How hard can a simple evaluation be?

Besides, who doesn't want to know what their spiritual gifts are, especially when you don't exactly know yourself?

On this evening, we all quietly answered our test questions. Each person individually evaluated her own scores and kept her answers to herself as we waited for the rest to finish. After completing mine, I quietly folded my test paper in my lap to prevent stray eyes from reading my score.

As everyone discovered their results, they began to chatter and survey each other's papers. I averted my eyes so as not to engage.

I snatched up my purse from the floor beside me and intently fished through it, jamming my hand inside, pulling out this or that. I tucked my head down as I looked for nothing, really. I gave the appearance of being busy, avoiding any revelations of the conclusion of my spiritual gifts test.

Why would those gifts be on the test? God, you see what church I go too, right? Aren't "prophecy" and "words of wisdom" what the Old Testament guys did? Um, we're long past those times.

I tucked my list into my purse and would investigate later. But I made the mistake of looking up as I slipped it to the bottom of my handbag. One friend's bright eyes connected with mine and she smiled. I froze for a second before quickly returning to my search for little nothings in my purse.

From the corner of my downcast eyes, I saw her bouncing up and down on the couch with excitement. She gleefully burst, *"Let's go around the room and share our top three!"* My face shot up. One hand was still buried inside the folds of my spectacular distraction.

Share our top three?

Out loud?

Everyone else seemed on board with this ridiculous plan as they stared back down at their papers, deep in thought. My heart plunged to my stomach, not sure I would or *could* share. This was a southern-brewed, super-conservative church, for cryin'-out-loud. They didn't take kindly to women as modern-day prophets.

Thankfully, the other women spoke first.

I debated speaking at all. As each person took her turn, a nervous energy vibrated within me. My throat felt tight. My hands shook. But even as a lead weight sat in my gut, I did not want to shrink back from God.

For too many prodigal years, I'd abandoned Him. And once I'd returned, He'd showered His tender mercies on me. He deserved better.

How could I deny His gifts now? Deny the confirmation of His works through this simple test?

If I hid behind silence, it felt as if I'd be rejecting Him and His good gifts.

My turn came. I don't know if I looked like the wide-eyed rabbit caught in a trap, the hunters' eyes stayed on it. But I started.

My bottom lip quivered before I could speak. I swiped at a tear as it raced down my face.

I silently motioned with my hand, a gesture of, "Wait." I tried to control the feelings that had surfaced.

When a prodigal, I'd created a tough exterior. Emotions did not come easily, especially crying. But when I came back to God, I asked Him to return to me, a tender heart. It did not come quickly, but it *did* return. And now, my tears were both mortifying and an answered prayer.

My gentle friends assured me that I did not have to share if I wasn't comfortable. But my hand again flew up in the air, pointing one finger up in a silent, "Hold on," as I tried to compose myself. I needed to do this.

I now realized I'd known these gifts all along. I had feared them, too. I didn't understand them. They seemed hokey. *They seemed manly.* But they fit me.

Deep down in my core, the gifts affirmed what I already knew. As much as I wrestled at that moment, He confirmed the truth.

That's when God nudged my spirit, *"Go ahead. Don't be afraid."* I would face my doubts and the invisible doubters as I decided to not shrink back.

My bottom lip trembled and in a shaky voice, I choked out my story. I told them my top three: prophecy, words of wisdom, and teaching.

Personal application & reflection:

1. Have you ever taken a spiritual gifts test? If so, list your top 3 here?

2. Have you ever spoken your God gifts or talents, out loud? Describe what you felt happen when you verbally acknowledged them versus staying silent.

Personal application & reflection:

1. What might you learn if you knew your God-given gifts and talents? How might that change your purpose?

If you've never taken a spiritual gifts test, you can go online and find FREE ones available.

*It is a **useful** tool for asking questions and inviting God to show you more about your creative purpose. Part of that purpose is two-fold, to intimately know Him better AND to better live according to the unique design He created for you. This in turn, glorifies God and can be a witness to others. It involves your personality, gifts, talent, and infinitely more than you can imagine.*

{11}

When You Accept Your God-Gifts

"Only as you accept your part of that body does your 'part' mean anything." The Message, (taken from 1 Corinthians 12:27-31)

I WAITED. I'D JUST shared with the small group of Southern Baptist women, the answers from my gift test.

I feared they would think me "charismatic." Growing up, I'd been warned about those kinds of people.

I chewed my bottom lip while my right foot bounced in rapid motion, a rhythm that keeps toddlers happy when on your knee.

What if they reject me? What if they turn against me?

But after a pause, I had blurted it out. I had opened my mouth and repeated the results—*out loud.*

For years, I had hidden from God. I'd walked away during my prodigal years and denied Him access. But, I'd changed.

I would acknowledge His work.

When you audibly share your gifts, you're exposed. You're splayed open for scrutiny. Fear of man tries to terrify you into silence. With exposure also comes responsibility, a responsibility and purpose to pursue the unique way He's called you.

When you *accept* the gifts that God has given, it empowers His work inside you. You become a willing conduit for His Spirit to be manifested.

The rightness of those revealed gifts settled in my soul with an affirming nod. I knew them. I knew them without knowing them, exactly. But seeing the gifts by name, they now carried definition and helped my understanding.

God had worked through Israel. They huddled in homes waiting for the Angel of Death to pass over. They faced a sea with an angry army pushing them to water's edge, They wandered in the desert and felt like "grasshoppers" in a land that *God had promised them.* His people did things they weren't always eager *to do (or go).* And yet He affirmed them over and over, *"Do not fear."*

In our flesh and in our imaginations, fear takes a swing at us. It is legitimized by the fact that God had to comfort His people when anxiety seized their souls. And still, He called them. With a Biblical history of people moving into God's purposes with trepidation, I find that I can too.

The gifting test operated as a tool. I recognized these gifts as His. But also, they are meant to be shared with the Body of Christ.

What the test did *not* do, was tell me how to use these gifts. In other words, I still needed to seek the Holy Spirit.

And as I've listened, my spiritual seasons have evolved. I've entered times where I felt fallow. I've homeschooled my two boys. I've taught other students and even writers. That is not the kind of "teaching" I first envisioned as a gift. In fact, I did not consider myself disciplined enough to be a teacher at all. All I knew was that I liked encouraging others, and teaching people stuff, is one of those outlets. Despite my doubts and lack of confidence, with God's power, it was possible.

Fear goes around banging on pots and intimidating us by being noisy and pushy. Fear strives for popularity, favor, and success in ways that are damaging to our soul. Fear silences us until we lose our voice.

I've admired the gifts in others while neglecting the one inside myself.

I thought myself not worthy of Kingdom work. Most likely, the enemy planted that thought and wanted me to believe it.

I talk about fear because the enemy uses this tactic to keep us from fulfilling our God-purpose and from using our gifts. Our flesh interferes too.

I've often felt unqualified. My history of misdeeds, mistakes, and worldly living stops me when my focus turns away from Jesus. Fear masquerades my deep-seated dread of rejection.

Besides, what father at Christmas time, gifts his children with presents but then tells them they are not worthy to open them?

We may not know, at first, how these gifts will factor into our lives. But if we seek Him with all our heart, wisdom and discernment will be given. God's mysterious ways can lead us like a good Father surprising and delighting His faithful children.

Over the last several years, when called out of my comfort zone, when fear tried to immobilize me, I sought God. And then I moved. No matter how my irrational fear threatened to harm me, I took a step.

I've had to rely and depend on, knowing God. Even though I do not do it perfectly, I've known Him through His word, in prayer, being near His Presence, and through others in the church.

Fear of man is terrifying and daunting and demonic. Fear of man is real. However, fear does not get the final word if God has anything to do with it.

The world says that there's strength in large numbers. But with God, numbers are not important. He equipped David to defeat Goliath. He empowered the handicapped, left-handed Benjamites with stone-slinging skills when it was preferred to be right-handed (Judges 20:16).

In time with God, our weakness yields to His strength.

Prayer changes how we see our situation. Speaking God's truth reverses the enemy's lies. His gifts are honorable and good. Our part in the Body takes an honest look at ourselves in why we hold back.

Where would my heart be without my blood vessels? Or my muscles without protection from my skin? How would I stand without my bones? What will protect my eyes if I had no eyelids? How would my mouth speak without a tongue?

This is how the Body of Christ works. Amputating one's self does not help us and especially does not help others.

I do not have to save the world. I just have to be who God called me to be, right here and right now.

I do not have to have all the answers. I just need to remember the One who is the answer.

I can recognize a fire in my bones and obey God. I can surrender myself to a calling inside. I can *grow* with God as I *go* with God.

I can decide to not let fear dictate my purpose or push me into safe and comfortable but *boring*, corners.

I can say out loud whatever God's called me to, even if I grew up thinking that doing such a thing (verbalizing a dream, a calling, or something promising) would somehow curse it. By withholding God's work in us, we also withhold God's blessing to the Body.

Instead, we look at those God-sized shoes and ask, *"How will my tiny feet ever fill these?"*

Only by God's grace.

Personal application & reflection:

1. If you've ever doubted your God-given gifts, what caused it? And how have you dealt with it?

2. How has fear of what people think held you back? What are some ways you could stretch yourself?

Personal application & reflection:

3. What God-sized revelations might God be showing you?

4. What insecurities have kept you from fully claiming God's gifts and talents in you?

What is one way you can be sensitive to using God's gifts this week? Pray and ask for Him to show you how He wants you to bless others by operating in the gifts He's given you.

{12}

How Waiting & Obedience Will Challenge You

*"Obedience is thicker than blood," Jesus, The Message
(Luke 8:21)*

HE GREW UP between cornfields in southern Iowa. Since a boy, my husband Vince dreamed of owning land. The desire was born the day his maternal grandfather bought a large wooded tract just outside the city limits of their small industrial town.

At the time, Vince's family lived smack dab in the city, inside a narrow, two-story house squeezed between neighbors. Two blocks away, homes with Gothic spheres poked the Iowa sky and verandas of Greek revival screamed grandeur to a street that lived up to its name: Grand Avenue.

But not on his street. Between rows of hard-working families crowded on smaller lots, his address housed people like his sheet-metal working father and homemaking mother.

Money was tight. His mom cooked creative meals. As a child, Vince mowed lawns and did odd jobs for pay. He delivered newspapers by bicycle. Once, he ventured several blocks away, more blocks than a child would be allowed in this day and age, to watch a construction project. Eventually, he was helping the workers.

But then one day, Vince flew in an airplane. He was fourteen at the time. And from that day forward, he loved flying. Yet, he never stopped thinking about that large wooded tract that his grandfather once owned.

Back when he was a fresh-faced eighteen-year old barely out of high school, my husband joined the Army. At the beginning of his career, Vince started as a tanker. It would be another several years of enlisted time, plus another few years of college before he would finally begin to live out one of his desired purposes--becoming a pilot. Sheer grit and determination propelled him to fulfill his passion for flying.

Still buried inside--laying dormant but alive—he held onto the idea of owning a farm. A wooded tract or ranch, it did not matter. From the time of his grandfather, the seed had been planted. Even after twenty-two years of military service, moving from country to country, city to city, Vince's dream never left.

When God's purpose takes root in us, it is often confirmed through others.

After we married, after we move back to the states from Germany, after he retired and we bought our dream house in Indiana, we both felt the call for land. I envisioned smaller parcels of ten or twenty acres. He imagined fifty to a hundred.

The desire emerged in us both. So we prayed. I carried nostalgic visions of what life deep in the country, far removed from the city, would be like. Even though I liked the idea, I also wondered if I was cut out for it.

I had dwelled in the city most of my life, content to live just on the outskirts of town and not much farther. Farm life appeared a lofty notion, one too grueling and arduous for me to sustain.

But despite my reluctance, I was drawn to it. I even daydreamed about it. I tried to picture how I'd fit into such a lifestyle.

When I imagined rural living, I saw our boys running carefree and closer to God's green earth than to man's gray concrete. But could this urban wife hack it? I wavered between romantic notions of farming and the anxiety of what tending large parcels of land would require from us.

Fear of the unknown and the unpredictability of farming or ranching played a factor. This new dream also ran counter to my extroverted, people-loving ways. But over time,

I accepted that rural living could possibly be a way of life for me, for us. Even though I considered the hardships, the desire for such a creative purpose remained.

As my desire continued to grow along with my husband's, we prayed about it. When the longing didn't go away or went unanswered, I resorted to thinking I'd erected some idol inside me. Then I threw names at it.

Pipe dream.

Crazy.

When the absence of clarity persisted, I assumed it stemmed from my flesh like a thorn poking at my side. I blamed the show, *Little House on the Prairie*, since I held fond memories of it since childhood. I told myself, these farm thoughts were nothing more than homage to Laura Ingalls.

I'm no Davy Crockett. I knew that. I'm not one to live in the woods or pitch yurts like someone I know named, Esther Emery. But everything I knew about myself suddenly became intersected with who I would one day become on a farm. For neither Vince nor me, or avoidance, or questions, or annoyance, or bewilder-ment could deter the pull we felt.

We finally determined it must be God's will for us.

We waved the white flag and surrendered.

"You haven't taken it away, God. If anything, it grows wild-
er and stronger--must be Yours."

Once we had accepted it as God's purpose, we walked in
the darkness of not knowing.

When would we go? Would we find our farm down the street
or across several states? How would we know which tract was
THE one? What if we messed up and bought the wrong one?

Even as we struggled, we waited. After a time that seemed
longer than necessary, our answer appeared.

In 2008, we were called to Texas for an emergency
visit to check in with my sick Granny on her farm.
Vince had been stationed in Texas during his military
service and vowed never to live there again. But after
seeing Granny's condition and realizing her farm might
be the one God was calling us to, we knew we had our
answer. We quickly packed our things and moved to that
Texas farm. We haven't left since.

From the time we felt that twinge of creative purpose
for a rural life surfacing in our marriage, it took almost a
decade for us to experience it. For my husband, it had
been three decades since that first childhood dream.

In other words, some creative purposes take time to mar-
inate. Don't give them up just because time seems to have

stolen them away. We may think we've been derailed, and our dreams may seem unrecoverable. But look again. God's timing isn't the same as ours.

A word of warning, too. Once you begin to walk in obedience, you may start with godly exuberance and excitement. But don't be alarmed when you land on the other side of your Jordan and find out you have hard work ahead of you.

Battles await. You think you aren't equipped to handle them. But you are! First, you have to oust the enemy, then break up the ground, till the soil, and plant yourself anew in a strange place.

When I found myself living on that farm, one that would require loads of sweat, labor, and patience while also shouldering the responsibility of caring for my dying grand-mother, I struggled to see the beauty of it.

We had arrived here with only the clothes in our suit-cases. Nothing was familiar – not routines, not meals, not communities, not friends, not even my husband, who had to return to Indiana for work until he could transfer to Tex-as months later.

At night when I tucked my boys into Granny's creaky farm beds, they cried for home – the one we would sell. I tried not to cry with them. *"Granny needs us now,"* I assured them with a stiff bottom lip.

Nights were always the worst. We had come here in obe-dience; that much was clear. But in those quiet, nighttime hours, the overwhelming task of forsaking our familiar life and becoming caregivers – and caretakers of this farm – haunted me.

Scripture warns us that in order to gain our life, we must lose it. I suppose we could sell it, too. Waiting on our God-dreams tests our patience and willingness to sacrifice. It can surprise us both pleasantly and *unpleasantly*.

But here's the thing: as the holes in our chicken house roofs became as numerous as the stars in the sky, I also start-ed writing again. I returned to my own creative purpose – mostly out of desperation. Yet it was a return all the same.

No one ever told the Israelites they'd need a life preserver to get to the land flowing with milk and honey. Yet they had to cross the Red Sea before they could ever hope to see God's Promised Land. Operating in your gifts and talents can have the same effect. I never expected it, but writing preserved me as we made this enormous move into what God had planned for us. Yet, even after we crossed our own Red Sea, we ended up on the other side questioning everything we left behind.

God calls us to give Him everything. As we learn more about who He really is, we might distrust that we really un-derstand what that means.

Or what if He gives us something we don't want? What if He requires too much? Will we be miserable and wretched?

Obedience sounds good on paper, like in those books of the Bible. Rarely do our own obedient steps toward God-only-knows-where appear safe or secure, however. When we get up close, obedience looks suspiciously like jumping off a cliff.

We imagine horrible sacrifices will be required of us. We build them up in our minds until we talk ourselves right out of obedience if we're not careful. *What if my children are taken from me? What if I have to do that one thing I know I could never, ever do? What if I look like a fool? What if people laugh at me?*

In fact, fear can ruin our lives. Our imaginations can serve as the feeding ground for doubts and anxiety if we let them. We cling to self-preservation, comfort, and immobil-ity. But we don't have to live that way.

Instead, we can listen to what God has been saying about our lives, and follow the creative purposes he has given us. We can replace doubt with obedience.

Personal application & reflection:

1. Is there an area that you're obeying God in? What is it? Or is there something you already know God is calling you too that'll require a hard obedience when the time comes? What is it?

2. How did it feel when you first got your "marching orders"? How did it feel after you crossed the Jordan, to the otherside?

Personal application & reflection:

3. Has your obedience been harder than you expected? What details made it harder?

4. Is there anything you're withholding to obey? What is it and why?

If God has been working on your heart about a particular obedience issue, take time to tell Him all your concerns about that issue. Express to Him in detail any hardships, struggles, fear, or gratitude. And then take five minutes to lavishly adore and dote on Him.

List what God shows during this prayer time.

God Calls You A Warrior

"This is for keeps, a life-or-death fight to the finish against the Devil and all his angels." The Message (taken from Ephesians 6:10-12)

SOUTH OF THE Israeli Plain of Esdraelon, a man crept toward his hiding spot, eyes darting east and west as he scanned the horizon. Several years back, his country had been overpowered, and now, even the workplace had become as dangerous as any battlefield.

Rabble-rousers and invaders covered his native region like invading locusts, a march of devouring armies that left a scorched, blackened earth in their wake. People were starving. Cattle had been ripped from farms. His homeland was under siege, and his fellow countrymen wore their oppression like burlap constantly picking at raw skin.

Only poverty and hunger remained.

But he had returned to his secret spot maybe one last time, ensuring no one followed him. He slid inside the wine vat safely out of view and collected the critical minerals for his family's survival. Then he took what little remained of his farm crop and tried to salvage it. His family depended on such precious grains.

With shoulders hunched and hunkered with the task at hand, he didn't notice that another man had been watch-ing from under a nearby tree. The mystery man must have startled him when he exclaimed from beneath the branches, *"God is with you, O' mighty warrior!"*

The beaten down man's head snapped to attention at the sound of another voice. He'd been so careful to secure safety in this concealed location. Now he feared he'd been discov-ered and was being overtaken by plunderers.

Once his eyes landed on the lone, mystery man, though, he recognized the angel of God.

"With me, my master?" asked Gideon, the man who had returned to his home and hidden from the oppressors. *"If God is with us, why has all this happened?"*

Gideon was more concerned about God being with him than he was about being a warrior. He had felt forsaken and had lived the last several years barely surviving.

"But God faced him directly: 'Go in this strength that is yours. Save Israel from Midian. Haven't I just sent you?'"

"Gideon said to him, 'Me, my master? How and with what could I ever save Israel? Look at me. My clan's the weakest in Manasseh and I'm the runt of the litter'" (Judges 6:13-15, The Message).

Gideon viewed himself as the weakest of the bunch, but God saw him according to His potential, not according to Gideon's own estimation.

Gideon would save Israel.

Gideon, the weak *"runt of the litter."* Gideon, the hungry, post-traumatic survivor, living under the terror of Midian. Gideon, who fearfully threshed wheat in a wine vat. *That* Gideon? A mighty warrior?

Where Gideon saw weakness, God attributed strength *"that is yours."* Where Gideon accepted his former hopeless, fearful fate, God redirected him to a higher purpose when He said, *"Haven't I just sent you?"*

Many remember Gideon as the man who feared for his life and *fleeced* God for answers. Even with God standing before him, he still wanted to know for sure, without a doubt, that God would deliver him and Israel.

You can't fault him for earnestly seeking answers. But look at what Gideon does next.

After six-plus years of starvation and being stripped of resources, Gideon asks for a sign, yes. But he also tells the angel of the Lord to not leave until Gideon can bring back a gift.

Not from surplus, but from his precious and insufficient supply, Gideon prepares a young goat and a loaf of unleav-ened bread. Not just an ordinary loaf, though: Gideon used a half a bushel of hard-earned wheat.

Let that sink in for a second. Gideon, a man who strug-gled to feed himself, used his flour to make a loaf of bread for the Lord, not to mention prepar-ing a young goat. Who even knows *where* the goat came from? This could have been his only reserve, given to the Lord.

Gideon may not have ridden out with a warrior's cry when he initially heard from God. But he gave God food from his scarcity.

Despite desperate times or lack of courage, Gideon believed. Even when he didn't know how war victories would be possible, Gideon must've trusted God's provision, even a little. He may not have believed in his own skills or had the confidence he could overthrow the enemy, but He pursued answers.

God looks beyond our self-esteem issues. He sees past our disadvantages. He goes beyond our history, circumstances, and our genealogies. He works in spite of the common wisdom of *like mother, like daughter or like father, like son.*

Our birth order, traumatic upbringing, or good deeds don't compare to the goodness of God's calling for us. He is not deterred by our self-condemnation or lack of bravery. He liberates His people and desires that we know him.

As Gideon prepared the offerings and asked for more signs, as he laid out the fleece one day and laid it out again the next, he spent his days talking to the angel of the Lord. Many times, I've missed this part: Gideon spent time *fellowshipping* with God. And through that relationship, his faith grew.

Just as Gideon's purpose came into focus through companionship with the Lord, so does ours. When Jesus returned to the right hand of the Father, He did not leave us as orphans. The Holy Spirit continues on with us today, reminding us, *"God is with you, O' mighty warrior!"*

How many times do we forget? How often do the trou-bles of this world rise like waves pulling us under, leaving us to fear for our lives?

There was another man who lived centuries after Gide-on. Maybe it was a freak accident that snapped his spine, but his legs refused to move. He had been confined for some time when his friends took him to a gathering. They'd heard about these healing events from others who said this man was the Messiah, so they all decided to attend. Who knew what might happen?

These friends had hope. Their faith propelled them to get there before the teacher left town. His reputation had preceded him, and they were more than curious to put these rumors to the test. But they arrived at the meeting late. All the seats were filled, and it was standing room only.

In fact, they were so far from the rabbi there was no hope of being seen by him, much less of getting their friend close enough to be touched. That's when they decided to scale the side of the building and lower their friend down through the ceiling.

A hush must have fallen over the crowd as the paralyzed man lay on the ground before the rabbi, unable to move. Jesus not only had compassion on him, he also took notice of his friends' faith. With religious men from the community looking on, Jesus said to the paralytic, *"Friend, your sins are forgiven"* (Luke 5:20, NIV).

This displeased the leaders. In their minds, they questioned Jesus' authority: *Who was He to forgive sins?*

"Which is easier: to say, 'Your sins are forgiven,' or to say, 'Get up and walk'," Jesus asked, perceiving their thoughts (from Luke 5:23, NIV).

Then Jesus told the man to get up, take his mat, and go home.

Physical paralysis isn't the only thing keeping us down. Plenty of things stop us from walking in our calling. The enemy comes to kill, steal, and destroy, and that might not look like outward destruction. Instead, he wages war on the battlefield of the mind.

The enemy aims fiery arrows at our souls. He tells in-sidious lies to infect our perceptions. He injects numbing agents into our hearts to freeze out the love.

But our creative purposes come from a relationship with God. And so does our strength. The joy of the Lord is that strength.

God has made you His stewards – caretakers of words, of people, of family, of gifts and service, of yourself, and of His Kingdom.

So what if you arrive trembling a time or two? Fellow-ship with God dispels thoughts of worthlessness. Commun-ing with God sharpens you to cut through the darkness.

Aside from an intimate relationship with God, you've also been given a mission. You've been given a battle to fight that'll lead others to freedom. You've been given a creative purpose like Gideon.

A mustard seed of faith, one tiny speck, goes a long way. We can bring our questions and insecurities before the Lord. Look at how patient God was with Gideon.

Have faith in the "strength that is yours." This is God's promise to you, too. Jesus longs to heal us. He wants us, too, to pick up our mat and go.

God is with you, *mighty* Warriors.

Personal application & reflection:

1. When have you ever felt like Gideon? Have you ever questioned why God picked you, the weakest (or least) of the bunch? Describe it.

2. Have you been too perplexed by what's been happening around you that you may have missed God calling you a "Warrior"? If so, do you sense Him saying it now and why?

Personal application & reflection:

3. How might God be waiting on you to ask Him for a sign so that you'll go to battle?

4. Do you have faith God will give you an answer? If so, are you willing to continue a relationship of asking and obeying?

Gideon fostered a relationship with God by asking Him to show Him signs. Each time, Gideon learned to trust God more. How might God want to show Himself trustworthy to you?

If you still struggle, pray and ask God to help you overcome your unbelief and build your faith.

{14}

When God Calls But You're a Woman

"God knew what he was doing from the very beginning." The Message, (taken from Romans 8:29-30)

RECENTLY, MY HUSBAND and I decided to research the scriptural context of marriage. We set aside what we knew from our own (similar) childhood upbringings and explored the topic straight from "God's mouth." We approached the Bible with a teachable heart, despite knowing what our childhood doctrines prescribed for marriage.

What we would discover was freedom. Jesus could (and should) be the "head" of our marriage. With Him as Lord of our lives, He sets the order. No more striving to fit into a model or mold of doctrines. It was simple--make Jesus the

Head of our marriage and our lives, and He is *more than capable* to teach us how to live that out.

Without even realizing the doctrinal burdens we carried, we felt a burden lifted. We felt emancipated from living by *formulas*.

What a relief to trust in Jesus! We learned to relax, no longer attempting to employ strict ideologies that only induce stress for both of us. We felt freed from the typical, damaging friction that a dogmatic doctrine creates. From a freed foundation, we kept our focus on our personal, individual walks with the Lord and released each other to pursue God.

The Partnership of Marriage

My husband and I consider our marriage a partnership, a team in the truest sense of the word. We respect each other's spiritual maturity and input. We listen to one another and weigh decisions by consulting each other.

We trust the Holy Spirit for each of our lives, being accountable to God for spiritual growth. We have confidence in the Holy Spirit's ability to use a man *or* a woman to accomplish His work, even a donkey when necessary (Numbers 22:21-28).

Extremism of any kind leads to suppression of one form or another. We've witnessed how extreme views often silence whole groups of people by race, ethnic group, gender, or other distinctions.

I've also observed how oppressive doctrines damage mar-riages. I believe that Jesus is in charge of our family. He's big enough to fill the shoes as Head of our marriage.

As a woman, I simply want to acknowledge the trust that God puts in anyone who's willing to be a vessel for Him.

God made both man and woman in His image. We are all part of the Body of Christ. We all have the same respon-sibility of loving God with all our heart, soul, and mind.

Bear with me as I review a familiar Scripture passage. I'm going somewhere with this but maybe not where you think.

In the Garden before the Fall, God created *them*, "male and female," and He commanded *them* "fill the earth and subdue it." But Eve had not yet been formed, only Adam. Still, God made "them." His plan was already in motion before Adam discovered his "helper".

God had formed water, light, and animals to fill the earth, followed by creating Adam. But look at what my husband pointed out to me. He showed me what God said *before* He created Adam.

"Then God said, 'Let Us make man in Our image, accord-ing to Our likeness. They will rule the fish of the sea, the birds of the sky, the livestock, all the earth, and the creatures that crawl on the earth.' So God created man in His own image; He created him in the image of God; He created them male and female. God blessed them, and God said to them, 'Be fruitful, multiply, fill the earth, and subdue it. Rule the fish of the sea, the birds of the sky, and every creature that crawls[c] on the earth.'" (Gen. 1:26-28, HCSB).

Not until Chapter 2 does Eve *physically* come into the picture. And she was not formed from Adam's foot or his toe or his shin, nor from his head or neck, but from his rib: the critical area protecting his lungs and heart, the part of his body which was neither the top nor bottom (Gen. 2:18-22).

At this time, the curse and wretchedness of sin had not yet entered in. Instead we have a picture of Jesus, who in Hebrews, as we know, became the second Adam.

"So it is written: The first man Adam became a living be-ing; the last Adam became a life-giving Spirit. 46 However, the spiritual is not first, but the natural, then the spiritual. The first man was from the earth and made of dust; the second man is from heaven" (1 Cor. 15:45-47 HCSB).

Out of a rib from the first Adam came Eve. Out of a woman's womb came Jesus. And from His death – from the One who was pierced in the side – came His Bride (John 19:34).

But what does this have to do with women and our gifts? First, God already had women in mind when Adam was formed. We were not an afterthought. We were not added to solve a problem.

We were part of the original plan. We, along with Adam, were created in the image of God, both halves of humanity, male and female.

Also, as the church, we continue bearing the image of Christ as His beloved Bride, both male and female. And if we are Christ's body as the church, then how did Christ, our head, treat woman? What example did He leave for us? Jesus befriended many women and called them to be disciples, even ones that weren't married. He never treated them as a less-than.

Jesus used woman in mighty ways; He didn't get caught up in theological debates, nor did He fret over giving a woman a job or gift. He didn't wring His hands at what people would think of Him because a woman fulfilled a duty instead of a man. He used whoever was willing: man, woman, or child.

I say this to encourage you. We can have confidence in God's amazing grace and mercy, which gives us opportunity to partner with Him.

God is not restricted by place or time, or even by our gender. He operates outside our human limitations.

God looks at the heart and goes for the most pliable. He sees the soul and says, *"This one, right here. Her desire is for Me, and I will fellowship with her, and she'll be mine. She'll do whatever I ask of her."* Or, *"This child. His heart hungers after Me. I will feed Him with the bread of Life, and he'll grow strong under My care. He'll become a man and will be My mouthpiece unto the world."*

If we need more examples, we can dig a little further to find plenty of vessels that God used for His glory.

Deborah, Leader of Israel, Prophetess, Judge

In Judges 4:4 (HCSB) we find Deborah, *"a prophetess and the wife of Lappidoth, was judging Israel at that time."* The nation depended on her because *"the Israelites went up to her for judgment"* (Judges 4:5, HCSB). One day, she sent for a man, Barak, the son of Abinoam from Kedesh in Naphtali, and encouraged him to be obedient to God and send troops to Mount Tabor as God had commanded him.

Barak, however, was not so confident. He went so far as to tell Deborah, *"If you will not go with me, I will not go"* (Judges 4:8, HCSB). So she conceded and went. Yet in the heat of battle – a battle that should've been won by Barak because the Lord had called him – a woman, Jael, claimed the victory by assassinating the enemy's leader with a tent peg.

God used two women in two very different ways. Through Deborah's reign, God brought peace to Israel for forty years. God did not hesitate in sending Deborah to encourage Barak, nor was He surprised by Deborah's position as a Judge, ruling over Israel. In fact, He Divinely appointed her.

Esther, Queen of Persia

After Esther became queen of Persia, King Xerxes issued an irrevocable decree, initiated by his servant Haman, allowing for the slaughter of all Jews.

Esther's uncle, Mordecai, sent word to Esther, begging her to take action. He asked her to boldly approach the King and ask for help. However, even though the King was her husband, strict rules of conduct prohibited disturbing the King without summons. Esther reminded her uncle, *"Any man or woman who approaches the king in the inner court without being summoned the king has but one law: that they be put to death unless the king extends the gold scepter to them and spares their lives"* (Esther 4:11, NIV).

By this time, it had been a month since Esther had even seen her husband. He hadn't called on her. He hadn't requested her presence. And he had already put to death his first wife when she openly disrespected him. Why would Esther be spared the same fate?

But in her desperation to save her people, Esther told her uncle, *"I will go to the king, even though it is against the law. And if I perish, I perish"* (Esther 4:16, NIV).

Not only did Esther break the law and go to the King, not only did she devise a courageous plan to uncover Haman's evil plot, while at the same time winning the King's favor to her cause, she also confronted her enemy face to face.

From Esther 7, we learn that after Esther pleaded her case but had not yet revealed Haman as a criminal, her husband asked, *"Who is he? Where is he—the man who has dared to do such a thing?"* With Haman dining in the **same room** with her and her husband, she boldly replied, *"An adversary and enemy! This vile Haman!"* (Esther 7:5-6 NIV).

Esther's audacious, daring, and heroic steps saved her people.

Miriam, Prophetess, Singer

After Israel's deliverance from the Red Sea, Moses' sister Miriam led the nation in song, as a worship leader who honored God.

"Then Miriam the prophetess, Aaron's sister, took a tambourine in her hand, and all the women Followed her with their tambourines and Danced. Miriam sang to them: Sing to the Lord, for He is highly exalted; He has thrown the horse and its rider into the sea.'" (Ex. 15:20-21, HCSB).

Miriam remained close to her brothers throughout her life, and God mentions her, along with her brothers, in His pleadings with Israel recorded in Micah 6:4 (HCSB). One can only imagine how the three of them led Israel, but God reminds the nation, *"I brought you up from the land of Egypt and redeemed you from that place of slavery. I sent Moses, Aaron, and Miriam ahead of you."*

More Courageous Women

The Prophetess Huldah responded to King Josiah with authority when he sought God's will from her. God had given Huldah a message, and she bravely proclaimed, *"This is what the Lord God of Israel says, 'Say to the man who sent you to Me: This is what the Lord says..."* (2 Kings 22:15-16, HCSB).

Anna, who prayed and fasted at the Temple, greeted the newborn Jesus, thanked God, and then she spoke *"about Him to all who were looking forward to the redemption of Jerusalem"* (Luke 2:38, HCSB). Now days, that might be called "preaching."

Also, Isaiah's own wife was a prophetess. Other women also had prophetic visions or angelic visitations, such as Jesus' mother Mary, her cousin Elizabeth, and Hannah, from the Old Testament, who pleaded to God for a child. Many of these women were sold-out devotees that never left God's side. And they did this while living in their own communities or raising families.

A Few More Thoughts

Finally, here are a few additional thoughts on women and their role in God's kingdom.

1. Through a woman's womb came the Savior of the world. Mary gave birth to Jesus, and through his death, all people, men and women, could come to God. Salvation came through a woman's womb.

2. Women exhibited their unashamed loyalty and love for Jesus. For instance, a woman extravagantly poured out expensive oil on Jesus' feet as an act of worship. In front of men – Pharisees no less – she wept and washed His feet with her hair even as she was ridiculed (Luke 7:37-38). She dis-

played courageous devotion to Christ despite men's opinion of her.

3. Women ministered to Jesus. Women provided financial support, food, and housing for Jesus and his disciples, while also serving the integral role of stewards of their own households (Luke 8:3).

4. Women were part of Jesus' teachings and meetings. Outside of Bethany, a woman named Mary, the sister of Martha, *"who sat at the Lord's feet listening to what he said"* (Luke 10:39, NIV). And when Jesus' followers waited for the Holy Spirit in the upper room with the twelve disciples, **women were there, too.** *"They all joined together constantly in prayer, along with the women and Mary the mother of Jesus, and with his brothers"* (Acts 1:14, NIV).

5. Women were known for courage: After many of Jesus' disciples abandoned Him during the horrible days before and during the crucifixion but many women followed Him and watched from a distance. (Matt. 27:55).

6. After His death, Christ first revealed Himself to a woman. *"Early on the first day of the week, after He had risen, He appeared first to Mary Magdalene, out of whom He had driven seven demons"* (Mark 16:9, HCSB).

7. Women equally worked in ministry. In Acts 18, a Jew named Apollos spoke boldly but inaccurately of Jesus in the synagogues. When a husband and wife team, Aquila and Priscilla, heard Apollos speak, *"They invited him to their*

home and explained to him the way of God more adequately" (Acts 18:26, NIV). Paul also mentions, *"Greet Priscilla and Aquila, my **co-workers** in Christ Jesus"* (Rom. 16:3, NIV).

Much honor also was given to Phoebe, when Paul concluded his letter to the Romans by mentioning her at the very top. He begins, *"I commend to you our **sister** Phoebe, a **deacon** of the church in Cenchreae. I ask you to receive her in the Lord in a way worthy of his people and to give her any help she may need from you, for she has been the benefactor of many people, including me"* (Rom. 16:1-2, NIV).

8. Women prophesy. As Peter, full of the Holy Spirit at Pentecost, attested from the book of Joel, *"'In the last days, God says, I will pour out my Spirit on all people. Your sons **and daughters** will prophesy, your young men will see visions, old men will dream dreams. Even on my servants, both men **and women**, I will pour out my Spirit in those days, and **they will prophesy'"** (Acts 2:17-18, NIV).

I could go on and on with testimonies of women who've served God and devoted themselves to Christ.

So what am I saying? What am I getting at?

Christ defines us. Why box Him in?

Why not be an open vessel? Because we are whomever God says we are. When it comes to His purposes, He works with all kinds.

Personal application & reflection:

1. What is your biggest struggle, if any, regarding your identity in Christ as a single person, spouse, or parent?

2. What do you sense God may be saying to you in your current situation?

3. Did you find parts of this chapter hard to accept? If so, which ones?

Personal application & reflection:

4. Do you have positive role models in your life that help you to stand firm in God's call? If so, who are they and in what way do they support you.

5. What are other ways God ministered through women or non-traditional methods in Bible?

God continually shows that He reveals Himself through willing vessels, regardless of gender or race (such as Gentiles). How might that challenge your beliefs?

Deeper look: Name 3 things that might hinder you from receiving a willing vessel of God in your own life, or in yourself. Then read scriptures related to those 3 topics and allow God to speak to you about them.

{15}

Looking At Yourself

"Look up, and be alert to what is going on around Christ—that's where the action is." The Message, (taken from Colossians 3:1-2)

HOW CAN WE know when we're entering a different season, emerging with a (sometimes new-to-us) gift like a bud ready to unfurl its blossom? This is where knowing ourselves and how God made us helps us better understand.

One of the hardest parts of living out God's calling is to know exactly what that looks like for us individually.

Just like there are seasons in our faith, I believe there are seasons, or cycles, in our gifts, too. According to God's bidding, we can rely on certain gifts for a certain point in time, only to later discover that God's equipping us differently for a new season.

Problem is, how do we know when to stay the course or move on and let go?

Sometimes, we look at how God works in others and expect Him to operate the same exact way in us, too. Or we mistakenly assume we should have the same gift as so-n-so, whether or not it fits our calling and personality.

Is discovering God's path for us really as hard as we make it?

When things are exceptionally slow (in life that is), I can feel that I'm not doing enough. Or I can run in a full-on sprint down the path I think I should be going, no waiting on God.

I can imagine that Kingdom-work looks like busy rab-bits bouncing and hopping in doing His bidding. if not careful, I can end up performing in my own strength and calling it God's work.

Other times, I've started out right. Traveled at a good pace, until I came to a crossroads.

Do I turn, sit still, or stay the course?

I've ended up trusting in my own understanding.

Or I've been fixated on the ground in front of my feet and forgot to look up. I have gone full steam ahead.

But when I've prayed about it and received confirma-tion, I've stayed true. I've relied on God's equipping for the right amount of time needed, no more, no less.

New ideas, challenges, and problem-solving projects en-ergize me. I'm attracted to activity. I also enjoy meeting in small groups or one-on-one with friends, family, and new people.

But I must be mindful. I need solace and quiet too. I have to make space in my soul to actually hear and be with God.

Many times along the way, I intentionally stopped jug-gling all the creative (or social-media) balls and discovered the world did *not* fall to pieces. I can let go.

Once I understood myself, how I tick and am wired, I could stay true to my calling and the One who called me. And the way He made me.

We were created in His likeness but also created differ-ently from each other. No exact replica can be found in the world.

Yet there is a simplicity of the Gospel message that we tend to overlook. But simplicity strips away the complexi-ties of the world and our busy minds.

When we think about what God did for us, when we return the grace at the Cross, we can build and rebuild our faith and our souls.

When I'm oppressed by troubles and tribulations, I can not produce my own worth and value. When I'm in a pit of despair, thinking happy thoughts will not replenish my joy. Focusing on me will not provide a positive and sustainable self-image.

God's Spirit alone does that.

When I veer off course, I can travel straight back to Jesus. I have not outgrown the need for the saving Gospel.

I need to be built back up. I need to be reminded of God's image and the way He created me.

I can go back to the elementary foundation of God's love, especially when times are hard or confusing. I can listen for His Spirit to speak.

We stay true to ourselves by staying true to Jesus. We're not called to be an island. We've been built to connect, to commune. We only have to look back to the Garden of Eden to know this. Each in our own way, created with varying personalities and intricate brains, we must discover where our talents and gifts fit into that picture.

As a body, we're meant to edify each other. By keeping our gifts and talents to ourselves, we deny the gift to others. By locking up the gifts, we deny God, too. We deny Him access to our lives. We deny His Kingdom to work through the gifts He's given us.

We deny His goodness by denying ourselves. We cut off our own lives from the very bidding of God's glorious and frightful work.

It would take the fingers on both hands for me to count how many times I've been stripped to nothing. Bare, exposed, and vulnerable, I've had to bring my wounded and frustrated soul to Christ. Ironically, when I felt reduced to nothing, it produced the greatest of spiritual harvests.

We learn much about ourselves when we reap after a whirlwind that has flattened us. Our spiritual and emotional fields, where once stalks stretched their proud growth toward an aquamarine sky, now destroyed. With our hand on the plow, we anxiously fret over the fallen crop. We survey the land before us and wonder, will God produce a harvest next year?

This is when we long for our forever home, far from human pain. We desire to leave this world-weary life and be with Jesus. Yet, not one tear, not one rip at the heart, not one hall falling to the ground revokes our calling.

It's easy to get discouraged during such times. However, each trial and tribulation leads us back to the cross. The Gospel greets us like a holy kiss. We can weep our sorrows and heartaches into the arms of simple grace.

Returning to the Gospel is the only place we find ourselves again. And any fire the enemy meant for destruction can instead purify us.

As hard as it is to silence our noisy lives, once we make a habit of returning to Jesus, the simplicity of what He did for us, the distance shortens and the walk eases into a soft cadence. The straightest line to staying true to ourselves is the one that leads us back to Jesus.

Personal application & reflection:

1. When was the last time you found it difficult to recover from a loss or hardship?

2. What areas in your own personal life do you have to be cautious of, otherwise you'll find yourself in a pit?

3. When you come against trials and tribulations, what do you automatically default too? Your own strength, isolation, condemnation, or pressure to perform better?

Personal application & reflection:

4. Do you have Christian friends who point you back to Christ and build you up in God? Who are they?

5. What ways can you help others back to Christ?

Romans 8:26-34 and Hebrews 7:25 mentions that the Holy Spirit intercedes for you and in the same way, Jesus, as your High Priest, also intercedes. What intercession would you imagine are being spoken over you, right now?

If nothing comes to mind, then ask God to reveal them, sit quietly for 5 minutes, and write anything the pricks your heart.

{16}

When We Embrace Our (Spiritual) Life

"Sin speaks a dead language that means nothing to you;
God speaks your mother tongue." The Message,
(taken from Romans 6:6-11)

I
F WE ARE to know what is God's will for our personal life, we won't solely find it in a sermon, 'though a sermon can confirm it. We won't find it solely with mere brute strength or through earthly knowledge or rote memorization.

But we can find it in the living, breathing, and active Spirit of God. He reveals the truth to our spirit through scripture or through confirmation by friends, family, preachers, or strangers.

A simple prayer that might be worth repeating could be, *"Here I am, Lord, use me."* But *"here"*? Where is that exactly?

Does here actually mean over there—for example, a mis-sion field? A big stage?

I've caught myself in a trap of comparison.

Instead, I force my "shoulds" to the side and look for God's path for me.

James 1:5 tells us, *"If any of you lacks wisdom, you should ask God, who gives generously to all without finding fault, and it will be given to you"* (NIV).

I have friends who received every bit of God's revelation, grace, and Spirit, from the start of their spiritual walk. For others like me, it's been more like an onion, peel-ing layer after layer of skin, wondering how it may burn or sting.

But when I return to the upper room at Pentecost, where I wait on His Spirit, He enables and guides me me (John 14:12).

I've tasted and seen how the power of the Holy Spirit fuels my life. It draws me toward a loving God with a supernatural sustenance. He directs my path.

As I continue my spiritual journey, I can expect to enter times of discomfort. The enemy *will* attempt to derail me.

But this spiritual life goes against the world. It goes against our flesh and our self-preservation. Yet it always goes with God. And when we're willing, we can take our calling and purpose to the ends of the earth.

We can embrace the Holy Spirit. We can enter His Pres-ence and allow Him to teach us. The Spirit leads us toward God's purposes for our uniquely called life.

Personal application & reflection:

1. To what have you said, in the past or recently, "Here am I"?

2. Has God ever surprised you and revealed a different path for you in His kingdom that you had imagined for yourself? What was it?

3. How would you describe the Holy Spirit? List what He means to you.

Personal application & reflection:

4. What situations or seasons of life caused you to pursue and chase after God?

5. How has the journey changed you or spiritually matured you?

In Samuel 7:12, the Israelites had victory at Mizpah so Samuel laid a stone upright and named it Ebenezer because God helped them. What Ebenezer moments can you name where God helped you overcome a battle, struggle, or wrestling of your soul?

List them and briefly describe those victories.

Additional Resources

Receive a FREE eBook, *Intentional Soul: 4 Ways to Purposefully Live and Love Your Life*, that can be downloaded here, by signing up at my website: **tammy-h-meyer.com**

Do you want a more personalized journey? I also offer Purpose-Focused Life Coaching.

Are you looking to move past being stuck or overwhelmed?

Do you want to experience more contentment and joy?

Are you wanting to set healthy boundaries or find the perfect balance that works for your life?

Do you want to overcome a feeling of not being good enough or not being able to me meet your own personal goals?

Would you like clarity that'll move you forward during a season of transition in life, career, or relationships (such as divorce, friendships, community)?

Do you want to be more intentional and purposeful where you expend your time and energy?

Would you like to overcome church hurts by focusing on how to start over again?

Do you want to have more focus, strengthen quality relationships, and enjoy life more?

Additional Books

Endorsements for *A God In All Seasons, Walking Towards Mercy, Grace, and Hope,* co-authored by TH Meyer & Amy Breitmann

"Transparent stories of both life's sober and glorious seasons!" ~Kim Hyland, writer, speaker, Founder & Host of Winsome

"An incredible poignant book!" ~ Jennifer Hand, Founder of Coming Alive Ministries and author of *Coming Alive at The Cross*

"For those who have been damaged by a hard fall or experienced a painfully long winter storm--this book will encourage you to nestle into "The God of All Seasons" because He is faithful, even in the waiting!" — Renee Fisher, Author of *Forgiving Others, Forgiving Me*

About the Author

 T.H. Meyer enjoys serene landscapes, porch "dates" with her husband, and Sonic tea with extra ice. After living in Asia and Europe, her family built a home on their Texas farm in 2008 where their two mini-Australian shepherds share the couch and ice cubes from the fridge. Tammy is a Purpose-Focused life-coaching strategist who also co-authored, A God of All Seasons: Walking Towards Mercy, Grace, & Hope, and is mother to three beautiful kids and grandmother to one.

In addition, she co-led and Founded an international ministry team with over 20 wordsmiths and artisans. This online ministry tenderly dealt with past church hurts and wounds where Tammy was the Creative Director, Coordinator, & Sr. Content Editor.. She also co-led an online women's small group with (in)Courage, The Consilium, and has authored several other books. You can follow her spiritual and writing journey on her website::T.H. Meyer: Purpose-Focused Living.

NOTES

36329366R00094

Made in the USA
Lexington, KY
13 April 2019